L'ATLANTIQUE

QUEEN OF THE SOUTH ATLANTIC

Les Streater

I would like to acknowledge the great help and assistance received during the preparation of this book from:

Richard Faber, from New York. Without access to his extensive collection and knowledge, this book would not be what it is;

My brother, Ron, for his help in the research and on the internet and for many happy hours together at Greenwich;

The Librarian and staff at the National Maritime Museum, Greenwich, with their archives and unfailing help and courtesy;

Stephen Card for his beautiful painting for the front cover, especially prepared for this book;

Steve Booth of *Atlantic Crossing*, a friend, collector and dealer of shipping ephemera, for items from his personal collection;

Lauren E. Kirk for her friendship and encouragment in the preparation of this title;

And to my wife, *June*, for her never-ending patience and support.

And of course, without the leaflets and pamphlets originally created by Compagnie de Navigation Sud Atlantique, and the ephemera produced by them, this history would have been so much harder.

British Library Cataloguing in Publication Data.
A catalogue record for this book is available from the British Library.

DEDICATION
In particular I wish to acknowledge the late
E.C. Talbot-Booth, R.D., R.N.R.,
to whom we and the nation owe so much

Early company promotional material – just before L'Atlantique *the company's famous coquerel emblem was finally dropped in favour of a more geometric design.*

Other books by the author:

Aquitania: Cunard's Greatest Dream	Maritime Publishing	1997
Queen Mary: from concept to delivery	Maritime Publishing	1998
Berengaria: Cunard's Happy Ship	Tempus Publishing	2001
Queen Mary: the first decade	Tempus Publishing	2003

Some pictures were of poor quality, generally due to their age. Rather than electronically 'enhance' them, it was generally decided to leave them in their original condition. Many pictures are from ephemera issued at the time by Compagnie de Navigation Sud Atlantique and from contemporary magazines. Strenuous efforts have been made to contact anyone who may have a claim to copyright of pictures: due to the age of some pictures, or for other reasons, it has not been possible to track down everyone. To any I have not been able to trace, I acknowledge their photographic copyright with thanks. Other pictures have been taken from either the author's collection, or the Talbot-Booth Reference Collection.

First published 2005

Tempus Publishing Ltd
The Mill, Brimscombe Port
Stroud, Gloucestershire GL5 2QG
www.tempus-publishing.com

© Les Streater, 2005

The right of Les Streater to be identified as the Author of this work has been asserted by him in accordance with the Copyrights, Designs and Patents Act 1988.

British Library Cataloguing in Publication Data.
A catalogue record for this book is available from the British Library.

ISBN 0 7524 2837 3

Typesetting and origination by Tempus Publishing.
Printed and bound in Great Britain.

In the early years of the twentieth century, the number of emigrants heading for South America was growing rapidly. It was never as great as for North America, but the shipping companies had one big advantage over the northern route – the demand for meat from South America was growing even faster, so suitably designed ships could operate to maximum capacity in both directions. French, German, British, Italian and others – all wanted part of it. The one thing most of them needed, to a greater or lesser extent, was some form of subsidy – either as a direct Government grant to build ships, or a guaranteed contract for carrying mail. One such was the contract between the French government and Messageries Maritimes (MM), for mail deliveries to and from South America, the Mediterranean and the Far East. This operated for several years, but Messageries became rather complacent about the security of the contracts and their renewal.

In 1910 a new company formed with the express intention of securing the mail contract from France to South America, the Société d'Études de Navigation (SEN), formed by a coalition of several French shipowners, two French banks and the Société Générale de Transportes Maritimes. The French government prepared tender documents so that interested companies could bid for the various mail contracts on offer: stiff conditions were attached, for example the number of ships to be supplied and service speed required were clearly stipulated.

Following a series of meetings between government officials and the two companies interested – MM and SEN – MM felt the conditions were excessive to cover likely returns on the South American service. It was agreed they would retain the other contracts, but the new company would be granted the South American route. Contracts were drawn up on 11 July 1911, for SEN to provide four passenger vessels, each with a minimum length of 175 metres (574ft) and capable of 18 knots, and an additional six intermediate liners. The express liners had to maintain a fortnightly service from Bordeaux to Buenos Aires, via

La Gascogne.

Lisbon, Dakar, Rio de Janeiro and Montevideo, with smaller vessels on the intervening weeks. The service had to be operational by 22 July 1912: twelve months was insufficient for the required vessels to be ordered, designed and built. This problem was compounded by the failure of the French parliament to ratify the contract until 31 December 1911. The ill-fortune that was to plague the company had started.

The directors of the new company moved swiftly. Orders were placed on 1 January 1912 for the first two ships. Chantiers de l'Atlantique based at St Nazaire was to build *Lutetia*, while Forges & Chantiers at La Seyne received an order for *Gallia*. The orders required both ships to be delivered in 1913. There was no way these ships would be ready in time for the start of the new contract: the directors were forced to look around the second-hand market to see what alternatives were available. In the meantime, on 8 February 1912 the company changed its name to Compagnie de Navigation Sud Atlantique, more commonly known as Sud Atlantique, with a capital listed as 15m francs.

The fleet was started when the directors decided to purchase the ex-Norddeutsche Lloyd liner *Kaiser Friedrich*. This unfortunate ship had been built in 1898 to run as a companion to *Kaiser Wilhelm der Grosse*. However she failed to meet the conditions laid down to the builders,

Kaiser Friedrich *under tow to Le Havre.*

Burdigala.

so NDL returned her. After a brief, unsuccessful charter to Hamburg America from October 2899 to October 1900, she was laid up for 12 years. A putative new Norwegian line considered her briefly but rejected her as unsuitable. Sud Atlantic bought her on 1 May 1912, for a reputed 4m francs (£165,000/$800,000) – a fraction of the original building cost. The directors managed to get a brief extension to the contract start date, putting it back to 22 September 1912, while they continued to hunt for second-hand ships which could also meet the contractual requirements. The next to be bought was the *Ormuz* of 1886, from the Orient Line. This was followed in following weeks by a further five vessels: *La Gascogne* and *La Bretagne* from CGT, *Tintagel Castle* and *Avondale Castle* from the Union Castle Line, *Staffordshire* from the Bibby Line and *City of Corinth* from the City Line.

Burdigala *awaiting collection. Initially she had a white hull with buff funnels and black tops, but was soon repainted with black hull, the funnels given black tops and the cockerel emblem.*

All these vessels needed reconditioning: none would be ready in time for the revised sailing date, leaving the directors to charter another vessel to enable them to meet the contract. This was the *Atlantique* from Messagerie Maritime: she made one round trip.

Kaiser Friedrich was renamed *Burdigala* (the Roman name for Bordeaux) and sent to Blohm & Voss for more efficient boilers to be fitted, then drydocking and sprucing up at Le Havre, before leaving for Bordeaux. On 26 September a private luncheon for around 200 invited guests was held on board to celebrate the start of the service.

Burdigala sailed on 5 October 1912 from Bordeaux to Lisbon, Rio de Janeiro, Montevideo and Buenos Aires, arriving to a large reception. Dakar was omitted on this trip as she was thought too large for the harbour. However, the round trip underlined the deficiencies of this liner, and major repairs were required when she arrived back at Bordeaux, principally to the engines.

Liger (ex-Tintagel Castle) *of 1896, seen here in Chargeurs Reunis colours.*

The *Liger* (ex-*Tintagel Castle*) was the first intermediate liner to leave, sailing on 12 October, followed the next week by mail ship *Divona* (ex-*Ormuz*). *Divona* suffered rudder trouble on the way to Dakar, and most of her passengers were transferred to the intermediate vessel *Garonna* (ex-*Avondale Castle*) when she arrived a week later.

La Gascogne was the next mail liner, sailing on 2 November, followed by the intermediate vessel *Samara* (ex-*Staffordshire*) on 9 November, the mail liner *La Bretagne* on 16 November and then the intermediate vessel *Sequana* (ex-*City of Corinth*), at weekly intervals.

Part of an advertisement for Burdigala *(top), and dressed overall.*

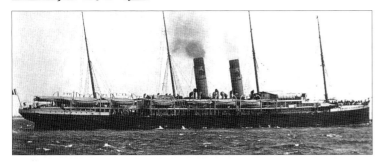

Divona (*ex-*Ormuz) *of 1886. The funnels had been raised by 13 feet.*

Garonna (*ex-*Avondale Castle) *of 1896.*

The next due to sail was *Burdigala*, but repairs still hadn't been completed. Again the directors had to charter, this time choosing the CGT liner *La Champagne*, sister to the two liners purchased previously. Unfortunately she collided with the Royal Mail Company's *Desna* in Lisbon, and was delayed several days for repairs.

Burdigala was still not available, so with no other vessels ready, the company failed to make any sailing the following week. On 28 December 1912 *La Gascogne* resumed the schedule: unfortunately sailing in dense fog she stranded near the mouth of the Gironde.

Samara (*ex-*Staffordshire) *of 1893.*

La Bretagne *of 1885.*

Burdigala *in the harbour at Dakar.*

Sequana (*ex-*City of Corinth) *of 1898.*

As 1913 started *Divona* was still undergoing repairs, so the directors again had to charter; this time it was the *Valdivia*, from the Soc. Gén. de Transports Maritimes, hired for some nine months.

By now the first ships ordered by the company were taking shape. The *Lutetia* was launched on 23 March 1913. At 579ft long and 14,783grt, with three distinctive funnels she was an impressive-looking liner. She was capable of nearly 19 knots, using a combination of triple-expansion engines and low-pressure turbines driving four screws – the reciprocating engines on the outer shafts exhausted into direct low pressure turbines on the inner shafts.

Following the launch of Lutetia, *tugs take her under control.*
Below: *Fitting out nears completion on* Lutetia.

There were four passenger decks and two small cargo holds, worked by cranes. Passenger capacity was quoted as 300 in first class, 110 in second class, 80 in third class and 600 in fourth, with a high standard of fittings and furnishings. Crew complement was listed as 410.

Completed on 15 October 1913, *Lutetia*'s maiden voyage was on 1 November 1913, from Bordeaux to La Plata. A successful outward voyage at an average 18 knots was marred on the homeward run, when she collided with and sank a Greek cargo ship, the *Dimitrios*, as she was leaving Lisbon harbour on 8 February 1914. Severe damage to her bows meant that she had to return to Lisbon; passengers were disembarked

Lutetia: *the music room and the smoking room.*

to continue their journeys by train, and temporary repairs were made to the damaged area. Once completed, *Lutetia* sailed for St Nazaire where permanent repairs were put in hand.

Above: Lutetia *resplendent in her new livery.*

An unusual shot of Burdigala *at the quayside.*

An early picture of Lutetia.

The second ship ordered by the company, *Gallia*, was launched on 26 March 1913. Completed in October 1913, she made her maiden voyage on 29 November 1913. The day after the launching of the *Gallia*, the keel of the next vessel, *Massilia*, was laid; the impending war in Europe first delayed the start of work on the fourth in this group, *Gergovia*, then caused its cancellation.

Similar externally to *Lutetia*, *Gallia* had three screws: two wing triple expansion engines exhausted into a single centre-line low pressure turbine. The masts weren't fitted with cargo handling gear: the hatches were worked by cranes. Sud Atlantique was unhappy with the engines on *Gallia*, and some rebuilding was put in hand at La Seyne after her maiden voyage.

At the same time her first class passenger accommodation, initially for 300, was increased. After most of the rectification work, she sailed on 20 February 1914, returning to La Seyne after the voyage for the completion of the work, finally returning to service on 16 May 1914.

The mishaps, accidents and delays to the ships and schedules was beginning to cause official alarm. It was also affecting passenger bookings which, combined with the repair costs of the ships, were putting the finances of the fledgling company in a precarious position.

Several meetings were held with various parties in December 1913, resulting in the Compagnie Générale Transatlantique (CGT) taking over as general managers, after the company's finances had been renegotiated. Four ships, *Flandre*, *Pérou*, *Floride* and *Guadeloupe*, were transferred from CGT to Sud Atlantique in the coming months.

A beautiful painting of Lutetia.

Gallia.

By now the directors had given up any hopes of using *Burdigala*, and she had been laid up again at Bordeaux. *Lutetia* returned from her repairs, and took the scheduled sailing on 16 May 1914, making a fast passage out and back. It was noted that although she left Bordeaux only a few hours ahead of Hamburg Amerika's crack new liner *Cap Trafalgar*, she arrived in Buenos Aires some 36 hours ahead of her.

With the outbreak of World War I in August 1914, many shipowners had their vessels requisitioned for a variety of purposes; Sud Atlantique was no exception, with many of its fleet taken.

Burdigala was brought back into service in March 1915 as a troopship for the Dardanelles and Salonica campaigns, then in December 1915 commissioned as an armed auxiliary cruiser, with four 5·5in guns and several quick-firing guns, based at Toulon. Later converted back to a troopship, under Lt Cmdr Rolland, on 14 November 1916 she hit a mine laid by the German submarine U73 – the same submarine that laid the mine that sank White Star's *Britannic*, on 21 November 1916, while operating as a hospital ship. The explosion was at 10.45am: she sank in 35 minutes, 2 miles SW of St Nicolo in the Aegean Sea.

Divona serving as a hospital ship.

Divona was taken over as a hospital ship in 1916.

La Gascogne was converted to an armed auxiliary cruiser in August 1914. This was not successful, and she returned to Sud Atlantique. In 1915, after three round trips to New York under CGT colours, she was again requisitioned, and served as a depot ship at Salonica for the rest of the war.

La Bretagne was requisitioned on 14 August 1914, and served as a hospital ship throughout the war.

Sequana was torpedoed and sunk by a German submarine on 8 June 1917, near the Île d'Yeu.

La Champagne stranded at St Nazaire on 28 May 1915 and broke her back.

Lutetia was converted for use as a troopship in August 1914, at one point bringing Russian troops to France, then ferrying troops to the

Two postcards of Burdigala *as a troop transport.*

A wartime postcard of Lutetia *although still in company colours.*

Dardanelles and Salonica. By December 1915 she had been converted again, this time as an armed auxiliary cruiser, according to some reports she was fitted with four 5·5in guns and several quick-firers. This did not prove successful, and she was quickly converted to a hospital ship.

Towards the end of the war she reverted to use as a troopship, including bringing American troops from New York to Brest. Soon after the Armistice in November 1918 she took French refugees from Rotterdam back to Le Havre.

Gallia was commissioned as an armed auxiliary cruiser in 1914, then became a troopship in 1915. She was torpedoed and sunk 35 nautical miles west of Sardinia by German submarine U35 on 4 October 1916, while taking 2,350 troops to Salonica. Over 600 died.

Another wartime picture of Gallia, *seen here as a troop transport.*

A rare postcard of Gallia, *in her guise of armed merchant cruiser.*

Floride was sunk by the German raider *Prinz Eitel Friedrich* near Dakar on 14 February 1915.

Flandre survived this war only to be sunk after hitting a magnetic mine at the mouth of the Gironde on 14 September 1940.

Guadeloupe was captured by the German auxiliary cruiser *Kronprinz Wilhelm* on 25 February 1915 between Dakar and Brazil, and was later scuttled by the Germans on 9 March, after transferring the passengers and their baggage to a previously-captured British steamer, *Chase Mill*.

In April 1916 there had been a surprise announcement: Chargeurs Réunis was to take over as the manager of Sud Atlantique, following its purchase of a major portion of the company's shares from Crédit Français.

In January 1917 Sud Atlantique bought the Hamburg America *Prinz Adalbert*. Built in 1902, she had been seized at Falmouth at the outbreak of the war. Initially renamed *Princetown* in 1916, she was reconditioned and renamed *Alésia*. Misfortune struck again: on her way to Bordeaux to join her new company *Alésia* was torpedoed by the German submarine UC69 and then sunk by UC50 on 6 September 1917, off the coast of Ushant.

Following the Armistice in November 1918, the company was forced to re-consider its position.

Divona was laid up at Marseilles: she was partially demolished in 1922, later being towed to Genoa where the scrapping was completed. To the end she was running on her original engines and boilers – 36 years of hard service, a testimony to their builders.

La Gascogne had returned from Salonica in a very bad condition, and was laid up at Bordeaux. After further consideration she was sold for scrapping in Genoa, June 1919.

La Bretagne was also in a fairly poor shape, but Sud Atlantique decided to have her reconditioned, at the same time renaming her *Alésia*. According to some reports work started on her in June 1919, but stopped again soon after, and she was laid up.

Lutetia was sent to La Seyne in 1919 for a major reconditioning following four hard years of war service. Her accommodation was later listed as 460 in first, 130 in second, 90 in third with 450 in steerage; she was re-registered at 14,654grt.

Liger, Garonna and *Samara* resumed the South America service.

On 24 June 1920 the French government signed a new mail contract with Sud Atlantique, which allowed for the discontinuance of the call at Dakar.

Left from top: *Salon, smoking room and first class cabin on* Gallia.
Above from top: *Smoking room on* Massilia; *dining room and grand
hall on* Lutetia.

Massilia, right, at Buenos Aires.

Massilia *at anchor.*

Above: Lutetia *in her later livery.; right:* Massilia *at sea.*

In 1920 Sierra Ventana *was handed over as war reparations.*

Under the terms of the Armistice, all vessels over 1,500 tons in the German merchant marine were to be spread amongst the allied nations, as reparations for losses sustained throughout the War. As part of this, in July 1920 the French government allocated the *Sierra Ventana* from Norddeutscher Lloyd's South American service to Sud Atlantique, who promptly renamed her *Alba*. This allowed the company to scrap *Garonna* in 1920.

Although the keel for *Massilia* had been laid at the La Seyne shipyard on 27 March 1913, and she had been launched on 30 April 1914, work had then been suspended while war raged across Europe. Following the cessation of hostilities, fitting out was resumed, as a quadruple screw design with compound engines in two engine rooms and three boiler rooms. Two small cargo holds were served by cranes.

The new liner completed successful trials between 23 September and 8 October 1920, during which she reached 20·97 knots. At 15,147grt and 600ft long overall, she was an impressive-looking ship. Designed with four decks plus bridge and boat decks, she could accommodate fourteen passengers in *grand luxe* rooms at the aft end of the bridge

Massilia, *looking graceful.*

deck, eighty-two in *de luxe* at the forward end of the bridge deck, three hundred and eighty two in first amidships on D and E Decks, one hundred and twenty nine in second aft on E Deck, ninety eight in intermediate and three hundred and fifty in steerage on E, F and G Decks, a total of 1,055, plus a crew of four hundred and ten.

By now *Lutetia* had returned from her reconditioning and resumed her schedule, sailing on 2 October 1920.

The maiden voyage of *Massilia* was on 30 October 1920, from Bordeaux to Vigo, Lisbon, Rio de Janeiro, Santos, Montevideo and Buenos Aires, completed in a record crossing of 9 days 19 hours.

Two new intermediate liners, *Meduana* and *Mosella*, were ordered from Swan, Hunter & Wigham Richardson on Tyneside. These two liners could each accommodate 100 passengers in first class, 150 in second, 150 in third and 400 in steerage. *Meduana* was launched on 30 September 1920 and *Mosella* on 3 September 1921.

Above: *Artist's illustration of* Meduana.

Above: Meduana.

Mosella sailed for South America in April 1922. Sud Atlantique's misfortunes were to continue, however: *Meduana* caught fire on 23 November 1920 while fitting out, and sank. This delayed the launching of Cunard's *Laconia*, as the slipway was blocked. *Meduana* was salvaged in April 1921 and completed, eventually taking her maiden voyage in February 1923.

Samara was scrapped in 1922, and *Liger* in 1923. Laid up since 1919, in 1923 *Alésia* (ex-*La Bretagne*) was sold for scrapping in Holland. While under tow the line parted near the island of Texel: she grounded and was later declared a total loss.

The company's bad luck continued. On 19 January 1925 *Massilia* ran ashore in dense fog near Bordeaux, although she was later refloated; then in 17 December 1926 she suffered a fire in the *de luxe* cabins.

Once *Mosella* and *Meduana* had settled down, *Alba* was transferred to the West African service of Chargeurs Réunis in July 1926, and renamed *Amérique*.

In an attempt to modernise the fleet and reduce running costs, *Lutetia* was withdrawn from service early in 1927 and sent to St Nazaire for a refit and conversion to burn oil fuel. Misfortune struck again: on 15 June she heeled over in dock during a severe storm and settled on the bottom, with extensive damage. She was raised on 23 June, and resumed service on 19 November 1927. In 1928 *Massilia* was sent for conversion to oil burning. At the same time the bridge was enlarged and other minor improvements completed.

In March 1928 *Lutetia* collided with the Lamport & Holt steamer *Balzac* in Buenos Aires, and suffered severe damage. Temporary repairs took 15 days, following which she sailed to Rotterdam for repairs.

A striking company poster for Massilia.

At some point in the late twenties the accommodation figures quoted for the liners were adjusted again. *Massilia* now carried 231 in first class, 71 in second class, 88 in third class and 456 in steerage. *Lutetia* was listed as 212 in first class, 114 in second class, 86 in third class and 500 in steerage.

In May 1928 Chargeurs Réunis took over the intermediate service of Sud Atlantique, acquiring *Mosella* and *Meduana*, which were renamed *Jamaique* and *Kerguélen* respectively. This meant that Sud Atlantique was now only left with *Massilia* and *Lutetia*, running a monthly service to South America between them. On 31 July 1931 *Lutetia* was laid up: in November 1937 she was sold for scrap. On 12 January 1938 she left Bordeaux under tow for Blyth, where she was broken up.

Massilia.

Massilia *at Bordeaux, in the harbour.*

Massilia, *seen here arriving at Bordeaux.*

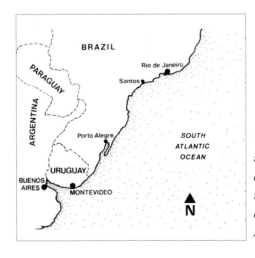

The same routes were used throughout the company's history: this map shows the ports of call on the South American coast.

An artist's impression of Lutetia.

An impression of Lutetia.

Company-issued impression of Lutetia.

A beautiful travel poster for Massilia.

Two fine drawings of Lutetia:
right at full steam,
left in harbour.

L'ATLANTIQUE

By 1928 the company was in a seriously reduced state. It only had two liners left, *Lutetia* and *Massilia*, and no intermediate ships, as called for in the original mail contract with the French government. Other shipping companies, in particular the Germans, had been using bigger, faster and more luxurious liners on their South American runs for several years: Sud Atlantique desperately needed to get back into the main group of companies servicing these routes.

The decline had been causing commercial concern to the bureaucrats and business communities around Bordeaux for some time.

With hull plating almost finished, L'Atlantique *is pictured on the stocks. Now almost complete,* L'Atlantique *still awaits her final painting.*

In February 1926 a meeting of the various parties involved had agreed to look into the situation. During 1926 and 1927 further meetings and discussions followed. As a result, in January 1928 an agreement was signed between the government and Sud Atlantique, for the building of two new liners and the development of trade between France and South America. It was ratified in April 1928.

Work on the first liner was to be started as soon as possible, with construction on the second to be started later, at a date to be agreed.

Another view of the yard as construction of L'Atlantique *nears completion.*

To cover the cost of constructing these ships, the company issued a series of bonds, guaranteed by the state. Two issues were made, in 1928 and 1930, between them raising some 305 million francs. The Budget for 1933 of the French Department of Merchant Marine provided a subsidy of 5,410,000 francs to the Compagnie Sud Atlantique.

L'Atlantique was to be built at the Penhoët shipyard at St Nazaire, under the overall control of André Nizery, a director of Chargeur Réunis. The keel was laid on 28 November 1928, with the launch date planned for 14 April 1930.

The Minister of the Merchant Marine, Louis Rollin, was the senior politician present at the launch, plus ambassadors and other dignitaries from the various countries to which the new liner would travel. There was also a large party of guests from the French government and other national celebrities.

On the day of the launch, there was an exceptionally strong westerly wind blowing, causing serious concerns to the launching crew, as the waterway was only just wide enough to accept the hull under near-perfect conditions.

A banquet was held, at which various dignitaries gave speeches about the state of French shipping, the French economy in general, the beauty of the new liner and the benefits it would bring to all the countries involved. The speeches were relayed by radio across France, and were also transmitted to Brazil and Argentina.

Following a brief religious ceremony in which the local clergy blessed the liner, Marguerite Cyprien-Fabre broke a bottle of champagne across the bow, and named the new liner *L'Atlantique*. However, the launch engineers had decided that there was no way they could actually launch the ship at that time, so the dignitaries departed. By the next day the winds had abated, and at 5.45pm the hull was quietly launched without further ceremony. It was towed away to the fitting out berth, where she lay for the next sixteen months, a scene of frantic activity.

Soon after the launch, it was realised in Bordeaux that Sud Atlantique were intending to run their liners from Le Havre. The company had started to advertise for crew in the town, and had begun

Control panels for the turbines.

A very clean stokehold!

interviewing. This made economic sense for Sud Atlantique: other shipping companies, in particular the French Line, were making Le Havre into the major terminal for the North American service, and the town enjoyed a good rail and road service with Paris.

Bordeaux was far from pleased when they calculated the downturn in business and employment that would result from the loss of the South American trade. Local business people decided to take action. They contacted the mayor, who contacted the Minister of Merchant Marine; he replied that Sud Atlantique was worried about the difficulties taking a liner the size of *L'Atlantique* up-river to Bordeaux.

Local people accepted there would be problems getting the liner up-river: *L'Atlantique*'s draught was 8 metres and overall length was

226 metres. Navigation and safety measures were going to be problematic.

They considered three schemes. The first explored taking the liner to Bordeaux on each crossing. The second looked into unloading passengers and cargo at a proposed terminal at Verdon, following which the lightened ship could proceed to Bordeaux for re-provisioning. The third scheme was to use the jetty already at Pauillac, roughly halfway between Bordeaux and the sea, for the unloading, until the Verdon terminal could be built. Work on the Verdon terminal, long-planned, was running at least 18 months behind schedule. In contrast the jetty at Pauillac could be improved and enlarged very quickly, and already had excellent road and rail links.

The starboard turbines.

Electrical control panels.

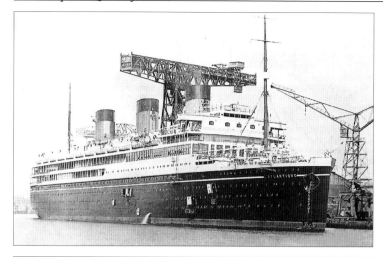

Finished inside and out, L'Atlantique *prepares for her maiden departure.*

The port authorities quickly accepted that the Pauillac 'interim' measure was the most practical. They brought in two dredgers to clear a new route from the sea, at the entrance to the Gironde river. This was given a minimum depth of 9 metres to ensure safe passage for *L'Atlantique's* 8 to 8·5 metres draught. According to contemporary reports, the new route was some 3,600 metres long and over 400 metres wide, with a depth of up to 15 metres depending on the tide.

The new liner was by far the largest and grandest liner on the South American route – her only shortcoming was her external appearance, compounded by the onset of the economic Depression.

The vessel was 717ft 5in in length, 91ft 11in in breadth and 53ft 5in in depth, and had nine decks. In designing the new liner, the builders had to balance two problems – navigating the Gironde River up to Bordeaux, and the depth of the channels at La Plata. To keep her draught down to the limits imposed by navigation in the River

Plate and the Gironde, she was designed with an exceptionally wide beam, compared to her length. As a guide, she had the same beam as *Île de France*, but was some 57 feet (15m) shorter. This gave her great stability and enabled the superstructure to be carried high, the height from the keel to the roof of the wheelhouse being nearly 120ft. Apart from the cellular double bottom with 35 compartments, there was a double shell abreast the engines and boilers. In the upper 'tween decks there were fire bulkheads and 13 steel curtains covered with asbestos. The fire-extinguishing equipment included sea-water, steam, carbonic acid gas and foam installations, the steam being for the holds and the carbonic acid gas mainly for the engine and boiler rooms and fuel-oil tanks. There were also a large number of portable extinguishers.

An impressive bow shot.

The vessel was provided with five passenger lifts, two baggage lifts, four cargo lifts and two goods lifts. Figures released at this stage stated accommodation for 1,238 passengers (488 de luxe and first-class, 88 second-class and 662 third-class), with a crew of 663. The whole of the passenger accommodation was of an exceptionally high standard, many of the public rooms being particularly spacious and lofty.

There was a double hull throughout, as high as the engine rooms and boiler rooms. This was divided into smaller compartments, used to contain 6,100 tons of fuel oil, 4,000 tons of fresh water and 1,400 tons of sea-water in the ballast tanks, double hull spaces and bunkers.

There were 13 transverse watertight compartments, with 38 watertight doors situated between the engine rooms, boiler rooms, propeller shafts, tunnels and accommodation. The doors were operated by a hydro-pneumatic system, direct from the bridge. Each door was fitted with a local control to enable any person trapped to briefly open the door to pass through before it again closed. Also on the bridge was a board displaying fire alarm indicators positioned throughout the ship, with a board indicating the temperature in various compartments.

The fire-fighting installation was well ahead of the statutory requirements of the day. There were 208 stations with fittings for sea water hoses, steam pipes, carbon foam extinguishers, and accessories for fighting specific fires such as in the boiler rooms or engine rooms.

The gleaming stainless steel surfaces in the kitchens.

The captain's private quarters.

In the upper decks many of the compartments had panels lined with asbestos for additional fire-resistance.

The bridge had all the usual navigation instruments, to the latest standards, including an ultrasound depth-gauge that could measure as accurately as possible the depth of water under the keel, backed-up by two electric depth-finders. There was a Brown gyro-compass with five repeaters and a gyro-pilot.

The propelling machinery comprised four sets of Parsons steam turbines, each set consisting of one high-pressure, one intermediate-pressure and two low-pressure turbines, developing 55,500hp in total. Sixteen double-ended cylindrical, multichambered boilers, distributed between two stokeholds, with 112 furnaces, supplied the steam. The boilers were oil-fired, working with forced draught and superheaters. There were two boiler rooms and two main engine rooms. Steam was delivered by two superheaters at 340°C and a pressure of $16kg/cm^2$, with an anticipated average fuel consumption of 500 tons of fuel oil every day.

Each of the propellers was driven by its own set of turbines. Steam could be admitted to either the high or low pressure turbine, and either of the low pressure units could be isolated if needed for maintenance or other reason. Geared turbines were expected to be more economical than traditional direct-coupled turbines. For astern running blading was provided in the intermediate and low pressure turbines.

Engineering staff comprised a Chief Engineer, 17 officers and 124 crew. Electrical requirements were supplied by three turbine dynamos of 1,100kW each, at 220V. An emergency electrical generator system was on the upper deck, comprising a diesel engine driving two dynamos of 40kW each, at 115V.

Throughout the liner all the cabins and public rooms were heated and ventilated by equipment from Thermotank. A separate fresh air system from Punkah Louvre supplied the kitchens, laundries and other working areas. There were 197 bathrooms and showers, plus 865 wash basins, 342 toilets and 65 urinals. Wastewater was collected in a central system and expelled through a bank of six pneumatic ejectors.

The hull was built of Siemens-Martin steel, to Bureau Veritas standard. High resistance steel was used for the side plating, reinforced decks and other areas. There were special frames for the large public rooms, and there were two expansion joints, one aft of the dining room and the other behind the grand salon.

Five cargo hatchways were fitted with two derricks each, operated by electric cargo winches. The cargo capacity of the cargo holds and 'tween decks was 3,580 cubic metres (126,800 cubic feet).

One interesting feature was the use of insulation between the hull and the interiors, much appreciated by the passengers when the liner was south of the equator.

Staff employed to handle the liner and look after her passengers included 30 officers and 600 men and women, spread between the bridge and engine-room and serving the passengers. In this latter group were 97 butlers and others designated to look after passengers in the staterooms, with 151 looking after the dining rooms and public salons, and another 54 which included such staff as hairdressers, manicurists, photographers and others.

Typical on-board stocks included 21,000kg of meat and poultry, 50,000 eggs, 130,000 bottles of wine, beer, etc. There were 14 temperature-controlled rooms used to keep the foodstuffs, ranging from -8 degrees for the meat and fish to +10 degrees for wine. A closed-circuit ionised fresh-air system supplied 14 provision storerooms, the

The gyro compass master, and repeaters on the bridge.
(loaned by Janette McCutcheon)

refrigerated 'tween decks, and the different cold rooms and water coolers in the rear of the ship. Cold rooms in the front part of the liner were served by 9 Hallmark Duplex machines and the pantries and two cold rooms for the luxury suites by Kelvinator. The kitchens occupied a space of 556 square metres and a volume of 1,416 cubic metres.

Two architects were chosen to oversee the interior style and decoration: Patout – who was to go on to achieve distinction on *Normandie* – and Raguenet et Maillard, under the control of Albert Besnard of l'Académie Française et de l'Institut.

The designers looked back at some of the famous liners of the past for inspiration. One feature they settled on was dividing the funnel uptakes for the first and second funnels, similar to the earlier German liners *Vaterland* and *Bismarck* (later the American *Leviathan* and White Star's *Majestic*), with the third funnel as a dummy. Instead of the traditional massive central uptake which intruded through all decks, the uptakes from the boilers were split into two, running up the inside of the hull before combining again into the funnels. This allowed the central, more stable area of the ship becoming available for use and enjoyment by the passengers.

The result was two of the most amazing areas on board any ship of this era: a magnificent dining room a full 35 metres long and 20 metres wide, on B and C Deck with a dome on A Deck, and the outstanding "Rue de la Paix", a central avenue of shops running 140 metres on E Deck, with shops, boutiques, salons, information centres and even a car showroom.

In total there were ten decks: Sports Deck, then A to H Deck, then Orlop. Above all this was the navigating bridge and the compass deck.

Immediately under the bridge were the quarters for the bridge officers; behind this was the radio room, then the sports area and tennis court.

The radio room was just ahead of the first funnel, and had three transmitters and a wireless telephone. The two long wave trans-mitters had ranges of 3,000 and 1,500 kilometres each, whilst the third was a short-wave system which could reach from Bordeaux to South America. The wireless telephone system was only for use by passengers. The telephone system on board had 150 lines available for use by officers and crew, and a second of 150 lines for use by passengers.

The captain on the bridge.

The bridge – fully manned.

The bridge deck.

The helmsman.

Above: *Two views of the tennis area as laid out. The billowing smoke highlights a problem of smuts on passengers' clothes.*
Top right: *An impression of the sports area.*
Right: *The seating area beside the court, with the promenade walkway above the benches.*

Behind this was the tennis court, a full regulation size, with spectators' galleries at the side, linking the second and third funnels. It could be floodlit at night, an especially attractive feature when *L'Atlantique* was in the warmer climes of South America. The shooting gallery was nearby.

Two views along the Boat Deck.

Above: *Part of the Promenade area. Below: the children's playroom.*

This featured national and international news received over the radio, as well as highlighting on-board functions, customs requirements and disembarkation notices.

Behind the printing room was a room set aside for children, including a dining area and a play area. The dining section was set up as a small-scale version of an adults' dining room, with small tables each with four chairs. The play area had a wide variety of games available, as well as gym equipment and other toys.

Immediately below this deck was the A Deck, or Boat Deck. The 24 lifeboats were organised on Welin oscillating (luffing) davits, unusual for the time. The twenty-two lifeboats were of steel, some 9·4 metres long and each capable of holding 88 passengers. There were two steel motorboats, equipped with powerful radio installations and capable of 6·5 knots fully laden. Also available was a whaleboat, and a small dinghy, plus a large selection of life rafts.

Quarters for the engineer officers were at the forward end of A Deck, plus the printing room, responsible for producing the daily menus, on-board notices and other material needed for passengers and crew, and the newspaper *L'Atlantique Sud*, distributed daily to all passengers.

Cⁱᵉ DE NAVIGATION SUD-ATLANTIQUE
CHARGEURS RÉUNIS
MAI 1931 / JANVIER 1932

LIGNES BRÉSIL - PLATA
HORAIRE DES PAQUEBOTS
(sans garantie)

SERVICE DES PASSAGES
3, Boulevard Malesherbes - PARIS

Nº 74

De nombreuses Croisières en Mer et des Voyages de Tourisme sont organisés pour 1931 (Programmes sur demande). L'escale de CASABLANCA est facultative au retour. Cet Horaire annule le précédent.

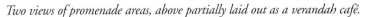

Two views of promenade areas, above partially laid out as a verandah café.

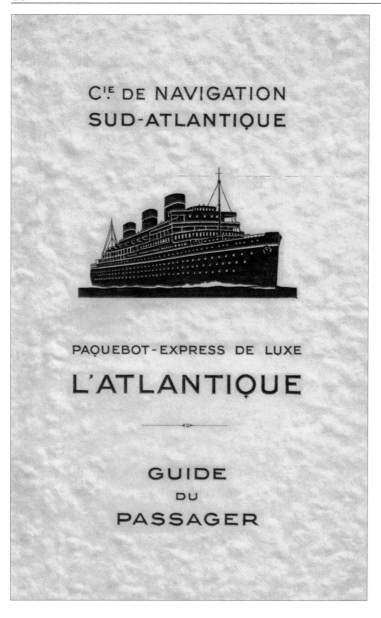

The next deck down was B Deck: the forward section of this was restricted to Third Class passengers, and included an open-air promenade area for them. The rest of the deck was for First Class: the Oval Salon, the Grand Salon or Music Room, a Café and the swimming pool.

The centre of the ceiling of the Oval Salon had a large glass dome, rising through A Deck and supported on ten columns of varnished rosewood.

Above: Comprehensive information was made available to all passengers as they boarded, listing facilities supplied and charges made for various services.

Right: A beautiful artist's impression of a gathering in the Oval Salon of typical First Class passengers.

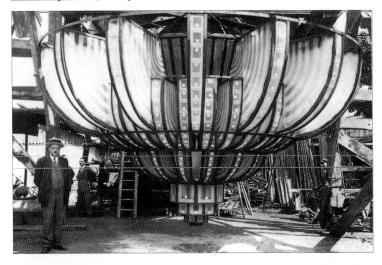

Top left: *The chandelier under construction.*

Left: *An artist's impression of a gathering in the Oval Salon.*

Above: *A pre-maiden picture of the Oval Saloon, showing the massive chandelier.*

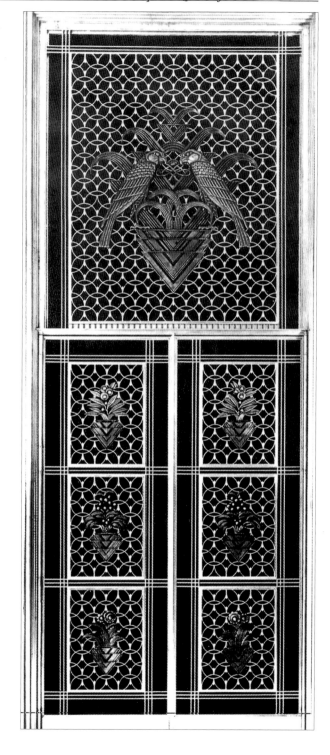

Above: *An early colour impression of the architect's plans for the Grand Salon. The finished room reflected these ideas very closely. Right: The ornate doors leading into the Oval Salon.*

The grand piano in the Oval Salon.

Looking across the Oval Salon to the Chapel.

The Salon featured a large Chinese lacquer frieze and an enormous chandelier. In the centre of the salon was an elliptical parquet dance floor, very popular in the evenings after dinner. At the back of the Salon were two small bars.

Between the Oval Salon and the Grand Salon was a Chapel, complete with marble altar and wrought iron communion rail. The chapel was beautifully decorated, and included large paintings by Lombard.

The Grand Salon, also known as the Music Room, was designed by Billard et Rousseau, decorated in pink marble and forest green, with a large ceiling dome on A Deck. It was 72 feet long by 66 feet wide, and 24 feet high. There were twelve large windows each seven metres high, fitted with panels of golden glass, which created marvellous effects. At night four large vases designed by Bagues gave indirect lighting, supplemented by wall sconces and ceiling lights.

Above: *A corner of the Grand Salon, showing one of the large urns.*
Below: *Vast lamps were placed in the urns in each corner of the Salon.*

The centre of the Salon was a parquet dance floor, while at the back was a Café, complete with a covered terrace and an American bar.

Running either side of the Oval and the Grand Salons was a promenade area, nearly five metres wide: the forward half was glassed in for the comfort of passengers in inclement weather. Further aft was a First Class verandah and a café bar panelled in macassar ebony and red lacquer.

Aft of the promenade area was a gymnasium, reserved solely for First Class passengers.

Two views of the First Class bar area.

Above: *The gymnasium.*

Below: *The Grand Salon. This picture clearly shows the height of the main windows on both sides, which made this such a beautifully illuminated room enjoyed by all passengers.*

The wrought iron doors to one of the lifts, and the ornate fascia, designed by Billard et Rousseau.

Looking through the doors from the Grand Salon into the Dining Room.

An ornate occasional table: in the base can be clearly seen the ventilation louvres.

The main First Class stairway from F Deck passed through the Hall, at the end of the Street of Shops, and on up to the Sports Deck. It was beautifully decorated in varnished panels of plane tree wood.

As well as grand staircases, there were five passenger lifts throughout the ship. Three were reserved for First Class passengers and one for Second Class passengers. These all went from E Deck to the Sports Deck. The fifth lift was for the engine-room staff, from A Deck to the engine-room. Other lifts included two designed for freight and baggage and two for the crew.

Two colourful impressions of the swimming pool.
Lower right: *The 1st class dining salon – before any passengers ever saw it!*

At the end of B Deck was the Swimming Pool, some 10 metres long and 6 metres wide. The area was complete with a thermal spa, massage room, with zones for hydrotherapy and sea-water therapy, plus a solarium. The pool had a terrace for sun bathing and deck sports, and the area could also be lit up at night for special events and galas. A fencing room was adjacent.

On C Deck, at the forward end was the Lounge and Bar for Third Class. Behind this were the luxury First Class staterooms.

Then came the First Class dining room. This could accommodate 370 passengers in a single sitting: the main seating area was on C Deck, and an upper area on B Deck. With the split funnels, it was an amazing 32 metres (105ft) long and 20 metres (65·6ft) wide: ten large windows each 6·5 metres high opened onto a side terrace.

Above: *A stunning artist's impression of the dining room, used in many company promotional pieces.*

Left: *A photograph of the Dining Room, with the tables now fully laid for dinner. Immaculate linen, gleaming crystal and polished silverware carefully placed at each passenger's place.*

A domed ceiling, with golden decoration, was 9·5 metres above the deck. The main decoration was burled mahogany, with large panels in Chinese lacquer by Jean Dunand, who was to go on to even greater artistic heights with his panels on board *Normandie*. There was also a separate restaurant, for those looking for somewhere that was a little less opulent.

The Dining Room, clockwise: the table layout; an artist's impression of a gala dinner; the enormous windows either side of the Dining Room, and the Grand Staircase from the Grand Salon down which passengers could make their entrance of an evening, showing off all their finery.

Above, clockwise: *One of the four panels that would all eventually be fitted in the corner of the Dining Room, seen here being prepared in the artist's studio.*

Right: *The four finished panels, seen in situ in the Dining Room.*

Below: *The final panel is from the Oval Salon, on the end wall above the grand piano.*

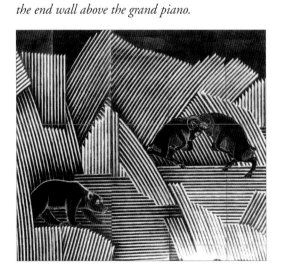

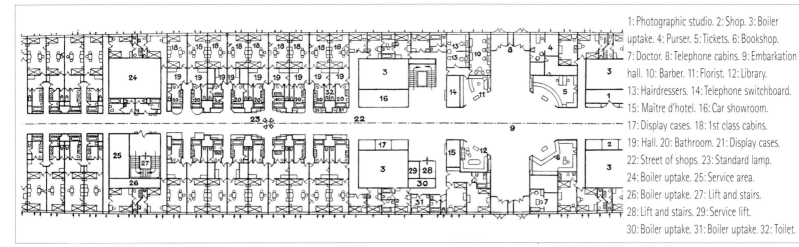

1: Photographic studio. 2: Shop. 3: Boiler uptake. 4: Purser. 5: Tickets. 6: Bookshop. 7: Doctor. 8: Telephone cabins. 9: Embarkation hall. 10: Barber. 11: Florist. 12: Library. 13: Hairdressers. 14: Telephone switchboard. 15: Maître d'hotel. 16: Car showroom. 17: Display cases. 18: 1st class cabins. 19: Hall. 20: Bathroom. 21: Display cases. 22: Street of shops. 23: Standard lamp. 24: Boiler uptake. 25: Service area. 26: Boiler uptake. 27: Lift and stairs. 28: Lift and stairs. 29: Service lift. 30: Boiler uptake. 31: Boiler uptake. 32: Toilet.

Top: *A deck plan of the area around the street of shops.*
Left: *Two views of the various display windows, with the highly decorative carpet.*
Above: *The information desk.*

On E Deck was the embarkation hall, and the famous "street of shops". Spaced around the octagon-shaped embarkation hall were an information bureau, a central telephone exchange and telephone cabins, a bookstore and a florist, all designed by Marc Simon. On the port side was a hair salon decorated by Billard et Rousseau. The central hall had white marble walls, with silver metal columns and Caucasian walnut panels. Balconies on C and D Deck looked down into the central area.

Top and right: *Two artists' illustrations of the street of shops.*

Above: *The automobile showroom beside the main staircase.*

Left: *An early impression of the information desk.*

The 'Street of Peace' was 5 metres wide, with a selection of 46 shops and display areas along its length of 140 metres, selling sporting goods, articles in shell or ivory, gloves, gold and jewellery, dresses, carpets, high fashion, lingerie, shoes, crystal, perfumes, furniture, and even automobiles.

Two views of the Second Class dining room and three views of the Second Class lounge.

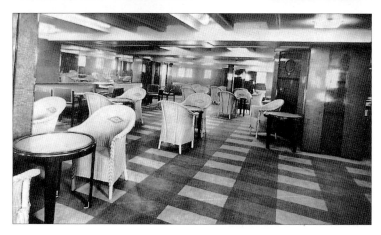

Left top: *Second Class bar;* Centre: *Third Class Dining Salon;*
Bottom: *Third Class Lounge.*

Aft on C Deck was the Second Class lounge and Second Class smoking room, followed by a children's playroom for Second Class passengers.

On D Deck were the Third Class dining room, kitchens for First and Second Class, and at the rear the Second Class dining room and Second Class staterooms. Third Class passengers enjoyed their own hall, dining room, bar and hair salon.

An artist's impression of a de luxe terrace cabin.

A bedroom in a de luxe cabin.

A lounge and dining room in a de luxe cabin.

The First Class staterooms ranged from vast suites to luxurious cabins. Journalist R. Chaveriat from Radio Paris described the cabin that he occupied for 4 days as he travelled from Le Havre to Bordeaux: *"A large antechamber with a wardrobe and baggage room. This antechamber opens to the right into a bathroom provided with the last word in comfort. To the left, the cabin: a true bed, a large sofa which, at night, can turn into a second bed, a table, 4 armchairs; an immense piece of furniture with all* sorts of combinations of drawers and pigeon holes, great mirrors that make the room more luminous. Fresh air is given with four ventilators that I can adjust, as I wish, for warm or cool air. Two large revolving portholes open onto the ocean. Lighting by an infinite number of lamps for all kinds of uses. Telephone connection with all onboard services and all the staterooms. The staterooms are all in various kinds of wood paneling with diverse fabrics. There are more than 50 possible combinations.*"*

The artist's sketch for the dining room for de luxe suite 29 on C Deck.

The artist's sketch for the lounge for de luxe suite 29 on C Deck.

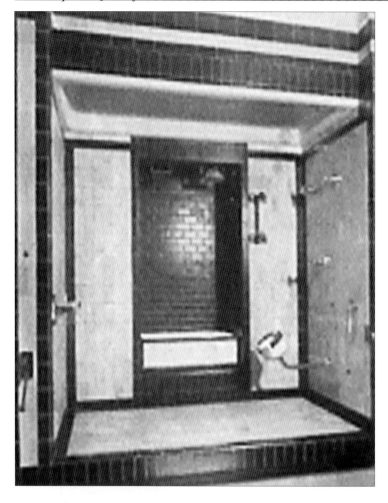

Above: *A typical en suite bathroom. Below: a de luxe suite dining room.*

Above: *A bedroom and suite in a terrace cabin.*
Below: *A cabin suite.*

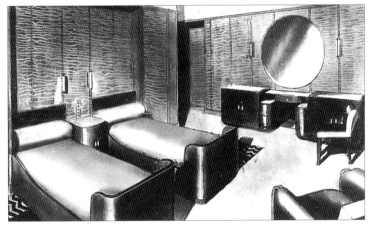

The luxury suites were in the most stable part of the ship, on C Deck. First Class staterooms were on C, D, E and F Decks; Second Class were on the aft sections of D, E and F Decks; Third Class were to the front of the ship, on E, F and G Decks. Officers were on A Deck and the Sports Deck, whilst the crew were on F and G Decks.

At the time of the launch, 160 passengers could be carried in the luxury suites, 302 in the First Class staterooms, 82 in Second Class and 660 in Third Class. There were no inside cabins in either First or Second Class. There were two luxury apartments, each with a bedroom with two beds, a salon, dining room, a private terrace 7 metres wide overlooking the ocean, bathroom, hall and baggage room. There were six "de luxe" apartments, similar to the luxury but without the private dining room or the terrace; 72 luxury staterooms with two bedrooms; 128 other cabins slightly less sumptuous for two persons; and 46 staterooms each with a single bedroom.

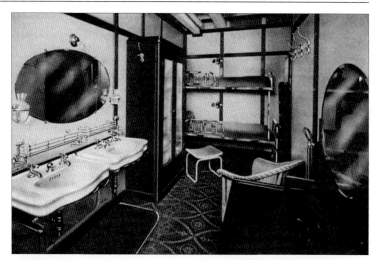

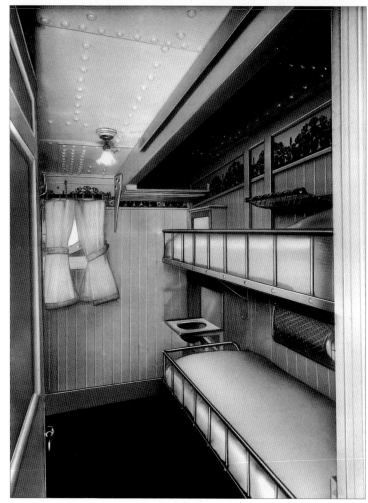

Facing page and above: *A variety of sitting rooms and bedrooms in first class cabins.*

Above right: *A second class cabin.*

Right: *A third class cabin.*

The arrangements for Second Class included 16 staterooms for two persons and 18 for three persons: plus a dining room, great hall, smoking room, promenade deck, game room, children's room, offices, hair salon, etc.

At the forward end of E Deck were many Third Class cabins, after these were Second Class cabins.

On 18 August 1931 *L'Atlantique* left St Nazaire, heading for Brest and her trials. Bad weather delayed these, so on 24 August she temporarily went into the main harbour. The size of the liner caused serious problems, and she had to be manhandled into the basin, rather than using tugs.

Once the weather had abated, *L'Atlantique* ran her trials near Groix, during which she reached 23·85 knots, well in excess of the 21 knots called for to meet contractual obligations.

Above: L'Atlantique *approaches Bordeaux for the first time.*

Right: *Docked at last.*

During August 1931 Sud Atlantique bowed to the inevitable, and *Lutetia* was laid up at Bordeaux, after a long, hard-working career.

L'Atlantique returned to Le Havre on 7 September 1931 to complete her fitting out. She then made a short trip off the coast of England, before cruising from Le Havre to Bordeaux-Pauillac. During the night of 23-24 September 1931 *L'Atlantique* traversed the passage, some two hours before high tide.

Above: *Two early sketches of* L'Atlantique.

Left: *Three early pictures.*

However, the businessmen and authorities in Bordeaux and the surrounding areas continued to press for the liner to come up to the main port, putting many arguments forward. They cited the advantages to passengers of arriving at a major town, and the benefits to the crew, all of whom would be able to reach their homes more easily at the end of the month's crossing.

Menu

—⋈—

Consommé en tasse

Potage Renaissance

Turbot Sauce Hollandaise

Noisette de Pré Salé à la Choron

Poularde de Bresse rôtie

Fonds d'artichauts à la Parisienne

Bombe Nelusko

Dessert

23 SEPTEMBRE 1931

An outstanding cover for a menu from 23 September 1931. (Courtesy of Richard Faber)

Major construction works had been needed at Pauillac to enable *L'Atlantique* and her passengers to be received safely. The jetty was rebuilt and strengthened, the roads were improved and resurfaced, rail links were upgraded; a new floating dock was planned. Electricity supplies and communications and telephone facilities were improved, and much of the equipment was modernized. A high-voltage line was run in to the area, sufficient to supply the cranes and baggage handling equipment and the heating and lighting needed for the terminal.

Hors d'œuvre à la Française

Langouste mayonnaise

Cœur de Filet de Bœuf à la Dauphine

Perdreau rôti

Salade

Asperges Sauce Mousseline

Fromages

Pâtisserie

Corbeille de Fruits

23 SEPTEMBRE 1931

Most menu covers from L'Atlantique *depicted prominent buildings in towns from the area around her home port. The selection of food offered at dinner was heavily biassed to pleasing a French palate.*

However, this reconstruction and development work was not fully completed until early in 1932, following which six electric cranes were installed, with a further six cranes held in reserve. Work was also put in hand on building a new, larger Maritime Station to provide the passengers with a faster link between the ship and the railway.

L'Atlantique at Pauillac, with the boat train alongside.
A night shot of L'Atlantique *at Pauillac.*

Four days before the maiden voyage there was an automobile rally in France for South American celebrities and their elegant cars, held along the Basque coast starting from the beach at Biarritz and ending beside *L'Atlantique*: luxury cars heralding a luxury liner. Following their arrival at Bordeaux, they were invited to tour the liner, after which there was a celebratory dinner and a ball, hosted by M. Vidal, secretary general of the Compagnie Sud Atlantique.

On 26 September 1931 a banquet was held on board *L'Atlantique*, hosted by M. de Chappedelaine, Minister for the Merchant Navy. Following speeches, Edouard Fauré, President of the Chamber of Commerce and Industry of Bordeaux, presented a bronze statue of the Greek god Dyonisios by Antonin Carlès. According to local legend Dyonisios (also known as the Roman god Bacchus) had brought the grape vine to the Bordeaux region to establish the world-famous wine industry.

On the same day, a radio broadcast was made by Chaveriat, in which he described a walking tour of the interior of the liner. He was on board during the brief cruise from Le Havre, and had been given full access to all areas.

On 29 September 1931 *L'Atlantique* sailed on her maiden voyage. After brief calls at Vigo and Lisbon, she reached Rio de Janeiro on 9 October, Santos the day after, by 12 October she was at Montevideo and finally on 13 October she reached Buenos Aires.

Sud Atlantique chose Captain Charmasson to be in command for her maiden voyage; he had many years' experience in the company's service.

The liner enjoyed good weather during the inaugural crossing. Tennis, swimming, sporting activities and lots of socialising were enjoyed by all. Every evening was filled with cocktail parties, balls, gala dinners and other entertainments.

Above: *Docked at Pauillac.*

Below *An early rare colour picture.*

Above: *A beautiful piece of artwork that the company used on promotional leaflets, brochures, posters and advertising material.*
(Courtesy of Richard Faber)

During this first voyage, *L'Atlantique* passed a major rival, the *Cap Arcona* of the Hamburg Sudamerikanische *(below)* and the two captains exchanged courteous wishes for a good voyage and a long career.

At both Rio de Janeiro and Buenos Aires celebratory banquets, balls and galas were held on board. Tours were organised for visitors, covering everything from the engine rooms to the wireless system and the bridge.

Right: *A famous advertising poster for Sud Atlantique, used to announce the start of* L'Atlantique's *maiden crossing to South America, and for later promotions.*

Below: *Hamburg Sud-Amerikanische's* Cap Arcona, L'Atlantique's *nearest rival for speed, reliability and luxury on the Europe-South America route.*

While at Buenos Aires, a charitable dinner for 300 was held on board to benefit the charitable societies of Buenos Aires. Each place was "sold" for a very high cost. At the end of the evening, there was nothing left but one small spoon from the House of Christofle's silver place settings specially made for *L'Atlantique,* each guest wanting a souvenir of the first arrival to their country of the ocean liner.

L'Atlantique then had a four day turn-round, sailing from Buenos Aires on 17 October, reaching Pauillac on 31 October. The round-trip had taken 33 days. With the return of *L'Atlantique* to Pauillac, Captain Charmasson retired and was replaced by Captain René Schoofs.

At a meeting after the inaugural voyage, experts again looked at bringing *L'Atlantique* direct to Bordeaux. Among the personnel at this meeting were M. Haarbleicher, Director of the Commercial and Naval Fleet; M. Leveque, Director of the Port of Bordeaux; M. Garnas, Chief of the Gironde Sea Pilots, and Captain Schoofs.

M. Garnas claimed that, under the right conditions, *L'Atlantique* could safely make the trip, allowing for the state of the tide, local fog, strength of the tide, local pilots, good communications between the ship and local authorities, and no problems with any of the machinery on board, with two dredgers permanently available

Below: *In spite of the torrential rain,* L'Atlantique *was welcomed to Rio.*

to keep the channel clear. He admitted that the primary problem was sufficient insurance on the liner during each trip. All participants accepted that the insurance problem would be the main

one to resolve. In mid-August 1931 the insurance companies had confirmed their reluctance to insure the liner for the passage from Pauillac to Bordeaux: they were not prepared to underwrite the risks. A delegation sent from the Port of Bordeaux had also met with the French Minister of the Interior in September, to see what help the government would be

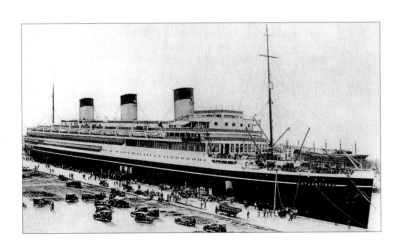

prepared to offer should it not be possible to reach agreement with the mainly English insurance underwriters.

Captain Schoofs stated that the present channel would be adequate, but he underlined the need for two dredgers; he also expressed concern about the frequency with which fog occurred in certain seasons. He suggested the construction of two jetties along the route, where the liner could be temporarily moored if conditions deteriorated during a journey. He acknowledged the financial and time constraints of this suggestion.

Later Sud Atlantique made a further valid point. Bordeaux was approximately 100 kilometres from the sea; for *L'Atlantique* to manage this in one tide it would take five hours at an average speed of 10 knots. The wake resulting from this would cause severe damage to the river banks and surrounding countryside, possibly submerging some areas by as much as three metres.

The sensible conclusion was reached – to stay with the original decision: to offload passengers and cargo at Pauillac, then proceed to Bordeaux for reprovisioning, before returning to Pauillac to pick up the next group of passengers and cargo. This would leave Bordeaux benefitting economically by supplying provisions, while passengers would be able to continue on with their journeys throughout France and the rest of Europe.

Conflicting arguments were now being put forward by the authorities in Le Havre, eager to increase their trade with the Americas.

Centre: *A medal presented to passengers on the maiden voyage.*
Bottom: *docked at Rio.*

High level approaches were made to the insurance companies involved, to ascertain their final position regarding insuring the liner to travel as far as the Port of Bordeaux.

In the meantime, following reprovisioning, *L'Atlantique* sailed on 5 November 1931, arriving at Rio de Janeiro on 17 November and Buenos Aires on 19 November. Also in port was French cruiser *Jeanne d'Arc*, completing a round-the-world cruise showing the French flag.

Returning to Pauillac by early December, *L'Atlantique* reprovisioned for the third crossing, leaving on 10 December and reaching Buenos Aires on 23 December.

On 18 December 1931 members of the authorities and organisations involved received a telegram from Pierre Laval, President of the Council and Minister of the Interior: "I regret to inform you that despite new

and pressing undertakings it was impossible to obtain from the French and foreign insurers that they would insure the risks run by the ocean liner *L'Atlantique* during the trip from Pauillac to Bordeaux: even limited to a single inaugural voyage." Various people and organisations tried to continue fighting the decision, but to no avail.

Below: *A beautiful colour illustration of* L'Atlantique.

Une suggestion :

Hors-d'Œuvre à la Française

Langouste Mayonnaise

Curry d'Agneau à l'Indienne

Entrecôte Grillé Bercy

Pommes Copeaux

Pâtisserie - Fromages - Fruits

Café - Thé - Infusions

Jeudi, 7 Janvier 1932.

CHAMPAGNE POMMERY & GRENO

1921	
Nature	avec le poisson
Extra-sec	et le rôti
Soc Drapeau	
Carte Blanche	au dessert

Menu

Sardines aux Achards - Maquereaux Ravigote
Haddock Mariné au Vin Blanc - Galantine de Caneton Truffée
Anchois de Norvège - Pâté de Volaille Truffé en Croûte - Caviar Rafraichi
Salades : Belge, Écossaise, Henri IV - Poireaux à l'Orientale - Olives Noires - Radis
Saucissons : d'Arles, Rosette - Salami de Milan - Crevettes - Thon à l'Huile
Melon Glacé - Galantine de Porc - Choux Verts en Paupiettes
-:- Petit Pâté Souwaroff -:-

Consommé Chaud et Froid
Crème Verneuil

Œufs : au Plat, Brouillés au Parmesan, Cocotte à la Crème, Pochés Mornay
Durs Farcis Chimay, Froids Carême
Omelettes : Salvator, Ciboulette, Paysanne, Parisienne, Chasseur, Princesse
Fines Herbes, Mascotte

Langouste Mayonnaise
Darne de Garopa Grenobloise

Curry d'Agneau à l'Indienne - Caille aux Raisins
Polpétine Piémontaise - Tête de Veau Ravigote

Entrecôte Grillé Bercy (15 m.) - Côte de Veau Grillée Maître-d'Hôtel (15 m.)
Mutton-Chop Grillé Vert-Pré (15 m.) - Côtelette d'Agneau Grillée (15 m.)

Cèpes Sautés Provençale - Petits Pois Paysanne - Courgettes Farcies Ménagère - Riz Créole
Carottes Vichy - Gnocchi à la Roumaine - Spaghetti Napolitaine
Pommes de Terre : Copeaux, Sautées, Purée, en Robe, à l'Anglaise

BUFFET FROID
Pièce de Bœuf Mode à l'Ancienne
Terrine de Bœuf Mode - Escabèche de Perdreau
Jambon d'York à la Gelée - Terrine de Caneton au Xérès
Galantine de Chapon aux Pistaches - Carré de Porc aux Cornichons
Terrine de Lièvre Royale - Pâté de Foie du Périgord - Jambon de Bayonne
Langue Rosée - Terrine de Lièvre Saint-Hubert - Pâté de Garenne Truffé en Croûte
Selle de Veau Rémoulade - Porc de Lait Criollo - Pressed-Beef aux Pickles
Aloyau Mayonnaise - Carré de Pré-Salé Tartare - Caille à la Gelée
Pigeonneau aux Primeurs - Foie de Canard Truffé en Croûte
Quartier d'Agneau Sauce Menthe

Champignons - Conversations - Gâteaux de Riz - Salambo

Camembert - Brie - Demi-Sel - Port-Salut - Gouda - Hollande - Crème de Gruyère
Roquefort - Reblochon - Emmenthal

Oranges - Pommes - Poires - Raisins - Pêches - Ananas - Bananes

Confitures - Biscuits Secs Assortis - Mendiants - Compote de Fruits - Dattes - Goïabada

Café - Thé de Chine et de Ceylan - Infusions - Yerba Maté

Service Maritime Postal
Brésil-Uruguay-Argentine

Chemins de fer du P. O.   *Cahors : vieux pont sur le Lot*

Paquebot express de Luxe
" L'Atlantique "

After spending Christmas at Buenos Aires, L'Atlantique *headed back to Bordeaux. Above is a typical on-board menu from this trip.*

Top: *Two views along the boat deck from the bridge wings.*
Bottom: *A game of tennis in progress, despite the clothing!*

Above: *Three pictures which clearly show* L'Atlantique's *lack of grace and style, at least externally.*

Arriving back in Bordeaux, *L'Atlantique* was sent for a refit and dry-docking. Apart from minor improvements required internally, the company had been concerned at smoke and soot falling onto passengers on the upper deck: in certain wind conditions it was rather troublesome.

After a series of discussions with engineers and designers, it had been decided to add a further 7 metres to the height of the funnels, raising them to a total of 19 metres, in an effort to reduce the soot emissions.

She was sent to the Penhoët yard at Le Havre for the necessary structural work, not only in raising the funnel structure but also in strengthening the supporting network and the inner flues from the boilers.

These two pictures, on pages 59 and 60, from Richard Faber's collection, clearly show the work in progress on raising the funnels.

A stunning painting by Roger Chapelet, used in several promotional pieces by the company. (Courtesy of Richard Faber)

On 27 January she entered drydock for her annual overhaul, leaving on 27 February with her new, improved silhouette.

Even with this she could never be described as a beautiful ship. The enormous height of the superstructure was emphasised by the black paint of the hull being so high. The impression was always one of strength rather than beauty.

By 3 March 1932 *L'Atlantique* had reprovisioned and departed for her fourth crossing, reaching Buenos Aires on 16 March. Her next departure from Pauillac was on 7 April, arriving at Buenos Aires on 20 April.

These pictures were taken during the annual overhaul at Le Havre, following completion of the work on the funnels. With her paintwork gleaming and the interiors spruced up, she was ready to return to service.

After reprovisioning, she sailed again on 12 May, arriving at Buenos Aires on 25 May. The next departure left on 22 June, arriving at Buenos Aires on 4 July.

On 20 July she returned to Le Havre for an overhaul. On 21 July she entered the drydock, leaving again on 16 August. While she was in drydock she was open to the public every day, with thousands touring her.

Returning to Bordeaux, she departed on 15 September, reaching Buenos Aires on 28 September, after another routine crossing.

The new funnels certainly improved her silhouette, but the lack of sheer in the hull and the paintwork on the hull combined to make her look heavy, ponderous and cumbersome.

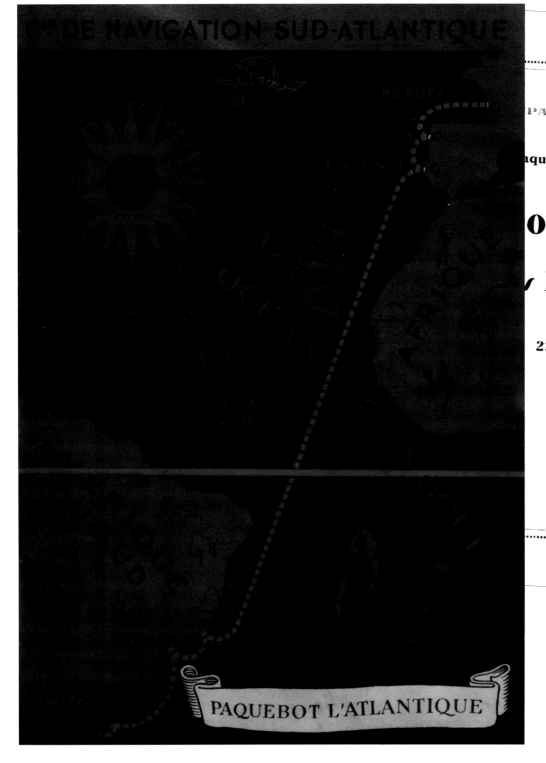

Cie DE NAVIGATION SUD-ATLANTIQUE

PAQUEBOT L'ATLANTIQUE

COMPAGNIE SUD-ATLANTIQUE

····

Paquebot "L'ATLANTIQUE"

PROGRAMME

DES DISTRACTIONS

23 AU 30 MARS 1932 ❖

PROGRAMME

MERCREDI 23 MARS

21 h. 30 : Courses de Chevaux dans le Grand Salon.

JEUDI 24

21 h. 30 : Séance Cinématographique.

Au Programme :

SUR " L'ATLANTIQUE "
AU PAYS DES BASQUES

VENDREDI 25
VENDREDI SAINT

SAMEDI 26

11 h. 00 : Concours et Jeux de Pont.

21 h. 30 : Courses de Chevaux dans le Grand Salon.

Danses.

DIMANCHE 27 MARS

20 h. 00 : Diner Costumé.
Bal sur la Terrasse du Fumoir.

LUNDI 28

21 h. 30 : Tirage de la Tombola.

MARDI 29

21 h. 30 : Courses de Chevaux dans le Grand Salon.

Danses.

MERCREDI 30

21 h. 30 : Distribution des Récompenses.
Séance Cinématographique.
Au Programme :
MONTE CARLO
L'ANGLAIS TEL QU'ON LE PARLE

Passengers on board L'Atlantique *enjoyed a variety of entertainments during their crossings. The above programme, from Richard Faber's collection, lists some of the distractions organised in March 1932.*

The next voyage left Pauillac on 20 October, arriving at Buenos Aires on 2 November. Her tenth crossing left Pauillac on 24 November, reaching Buenos Aires on 7 December and returning to Bordeaux on 29 December 1932.

Following New Year celebrations, *L'Atlantique* prepared to leave port, heading for a refit at Le Havre.

Author's Note: There have been several versions of following events, some contemporaneous, some written years later, some written with French national or political interests at heart. I have tried to find a route through the conflicting details. Much of the following story is pieced together from radio messages and press reports published at the time, survivors' tales, and reports from salvage assessors and an investigation into possible sabotage and arson. Radio messages and press association reports are shown indented and in a different typeface; magazine and newspaper articles are shown in tinted boxes, with accreditations where known. The textual interpretation is mine. Some readers may disagree with my interpretation of events: anyone with conflicting evidence should forward it for consideration in revisions for a second edition.

At 6.45am on Tuesday, 3 January 1933, *L'Atlantique* eased away from the Pauillac terminal, under the command of Captain Schoofs. There were no passengers or cargo, and a reduced crew of 229. These were mainly engine-room and boiler-room crew, plus the bridge crew. There was a light fog on the river that morning, although the weather forecast predicted strong winds and heavy seas.

As *L'Atlantique* turned into the English Channel, the weather began to deteriorate: with the liner running very light, the heavy waves began to make her roll to an increasing degree. The pitching and rolling increased as the evening wore on, and even the engine-room staff were finding it difficult to move around.

By late evening Schoofs was resting, fully clothed, in a small cabin behind the bridge. Gaston was in command, along with the officer of the watch: Gaston retired at 10.00pm, leaving the experienced officer of the watch in control.

At 4.30am seaman Raimandia noticed smoke coming from cabin 232 on E Deck. He alerted seamen Renard and Faletti, who were on night watch. They immediately raised the fire alarm, and notified the

An early version of events was published but later repudiated: A graphic account of how the fire was discovered was given by a telephonist who, wakeful, went up to watch his comrade on duty. He watched a man sweeping a corridor. "What a dust you are making," he said, but he soon noticed that the dust was smoke coming from beneath the door of cabin 232, in which the mattresses were stored. When the door was opened a stifling cloud poured out. No doubt was possible and the alarm was given.

bridge. As soon as the alarm bells rang, Schoofs and Gaston returned to the bridge. After being advised of the situation, they headed for the site of the fire to assess the dangers. By the time they had taken the lift down to E Deck, smoke was already filling the corridor.

The firefighting team arrived, armed with fire extinguishers, and everyone present donned facemasks. The doors to Cabins E232 and E234 were opened, but already the smoke inside was too dense to allow the firefighters inside. Schoofs ordered all adjacent doors and portholes opened in an attempt to dissipate the smoke, so they could assess the risks and the damage.

Around 4.30am Engineering Officer Paul Dejoie had noticed smoke in the engine-room. He sent his deputy off to investigate, who came back after failing to detect anything. Dejoie then looked for himself, and found that the area storing fuel oil above the boilers was full of smoke, although the deck did not seem particularly hot. He therefore assumed the source of the smoke was higher up. When the alarm bells rang he notified Emile Durance, who was in charge of the engineering night watch, of the smoke.

Other fires were already developing in the First Class Hall and on C Deck, and he despatched various crew members to tackle these. By 5.00am it initially appeared that the various fires were under control.

By this time Schoofs had returned to the bridge. Gaston, who had remained below on E Deck, rang through to advise him that the fires were now spreading further and quite rapidly.

Schoofs increased speed and changed direction slightly in order to reduce the pitching and rolling, so the men fighting the fires would find it easier to move around. He then called in all available members of the crew to assist with the firefighting. In spite of their face masks, they were all being overcome by the smoke. Varnish on the wall panels was spontaneously igniting and the flames were jumping past his men.

The fire was spreading unchecked. The central street acted as a funnel for the flames, as they leapt from shop to shop. Carpets and decorative panels fed the fire, the nitro-cellulose paints and varnishes so lovingly applied only a short time before now hastened the demise of the ship. A lack of specialised fire-fighting suits and major equipment restricted the efforts of the crew, who were becoming exhausted. Decks and hull plates were buckling and warping with the heat.

An engineer, Jean Dupin, had boarded *L'Atlantique* at Bordeaux, charged with supervising the overhaul at Le Havre. It was suddenly realised that no-one had seen him since the crisis developed.

Gaston volunteered to head back down to Dupin's cabin and check on him. Blinded by the smoke, and choking through his handkerchief, he managed to reach the door and rouse Dupin, before collapsing and being dragged into the cabin. The spreading fire made returning along the same route impossible: the only alternative was to escape via the porthole. Fortunately the internal telephones were still working, so they rang through to the bridge and asked someone to drop a ladder down the outside of the hull to the porthole. They each managed to squeeze through and climb the ladder back to the bridge.

Schoofs rang down to the engine room and ordered the engines stopped, as the winds were now fanning the flames to even greater heights. Flames could be seen coming from the forward section, indicating either that the fire was spreading faster than they had realised, or that another fire had broken out. The heat had shattered the huge windows of the great salons, and the inrushing air was feeding the fire.

The crew, led by Hector Courrie, were still fighting the worst of the fires, pumping gallons of seawater in, as the engineers fought to keep the pumps running. Slowly the great liner was developing a list, as the firefighters continued pumping water on board, until the list reached 15 degrees. The forward starboard shaft bossing and propeller was now clear of the water. As crewmen dropped with exhaustion and crawled off to find fresh air, so others came forward to take their places.

Courrie returned into the fire several times to rescue men who had collapsed and were incapable of crawling away from the advancing fire. He then told his crew to turn their hoses on him and keep him sprayed down as he went back into the fire once more in an attempt to close a fire door to keep a section sealed off. He didn't return.

St Catherine's Point received the following messages from Niton Wireless Station: "Following received from German motor vessel *Ruhr* at 6.55am: One mile from us is large vessel in flames. We are proceeding and launching our lifeboats. Our position lat. 49°30′N, long. 3°17′W."

"7.35am, name of ship in flames French liner *L'Atlantique*, moving for repairs; no passengers on board but large crew. Crew being taken off by German motor vessel *Ruhr*."

The officers on the bridge of *L'Atlantique* could see the approaching navigation lights of ships that had seen the flames: by now it was

7.45am, and dawn was breaking on the drama. With a final look round, Schoofs admitted defeat, and ordered "Abandon Ship".

The smoke and heat on the port side, coupled with the strong south-easterly winds and starboard list, meant that the lifeboats on that side were not available, so the crew assembled at the lifeboats on the starboard side. In spite of the list, now nearing twenty degrees, the crew started to leave using lifeboats 17, 19, 21 and 23.

The first of the rescue ships to arrive had been Hamburg Amerika's *Ruhr*, joined soon after by the Dutch cargo ship *Achilles*, then *Ford Castle, Falmouth* and *Erato*, and finally North German Lloyd's *Sierra Salvada*. Several launched their own lifeboats to assist the exhausted men from *L'Atlantique*.

The next message relayed from Niton reported: 8.18am, motor vessel *Ruhr* has taken off about 80 of crew of about 250 of steamer *L'Atlantique*. British steamer *Ford Castle* quarter mile from position, proceeding to assist."

Guernsey reported: "French liner *L'Atlantique* reported on fire and abandoned 23 miles WNW of Hanois Lighthouse."

Shortly after, Reuters news agency carried a story from Havre: "The super liner *L'Atlantique*, which was proceeding without passengers from Pauillac to Havre, caught fire between Cherbourg and Havre, and was abandoned by the crew. The minesweeper *Pollux* and the tug *Barfleur* have been sent from Cherbourg, and two tugs with fire-fighting apparatus have been sent from Havre. The powerful tug *Minotaure* is on her way to the spot from Brest."

In the meantime the "Abandon Ship" signal had been passed to the engine room, where Paul Dejoie and Emile Durance assessed the risks to the situation. Their first decision was to shut down the boilers and the oil burners to reduce the risk of an explosion. However, the smoke was by now too dense to enable them to reach the forward boiler room where other members of the crew were still working. Dejoie shut off the ventilation system, alerting the men in the forward boiler room to the danger, and they left immediately.

Most of the engineering officers and crew assembled in the engine room, except for three of the crew, who got lost in the smoke and were later found to have died through smoke inhalation. Using a tunnel at the rear of the room, the rest arrived near the stern.

Paul Dejoie, with about 20 men from his crew, gathered around lifeboat 15, which was swung out ready for launching. The men assembled in the boat, and Dejoie started the winch to lower the life-boat. The fire leapt forward, forcing Dejoie to retreat from the winch, and slide down a cable into the boat, as it hung suspended halfway down the side of the hull. The fire gathered force on the boat deck, until one of the cables burned through, tipping the boat on its end and dropping the men aboard into the sea about thirty feet below.

Other members of the crew had started to jump overboard; eventually all were picked up by the lifeboats from the surrounding ships. Most were taken to the Dutch cargo ship *Achilles*, where they were thawed out and dressed in dry clothes. Relatively few were injured, mostly with minor burns and grazes. A few were suffering from the effects of smoke inhalation, but these soon recovered.

As daylight grew, *Achilles* realised that there were still several people onboard, clustered on the forecastle, including Schoofs, Gaston, the ship's doctor and a number of crewmen. Most couldn't swim, and only three had lifejackets.

To set an example, Gustave Gaston climbed the rails and jumped into the sea: reappearing soon after, he was quickly collected by a lifeboat from the *Ford Castle*.

Once the captain of the *Achilles* had been assured by Dejoie that there was virtually no risk of an explosion as the fuel oil to the boilers had been turned off, he agreed to get closer to the stricken liner. As the lifeboats from *Achilles* approached, the crew left on the forecastle slid down a variety of ropes into the sea, from where they were promptly picked up by the waiting lifeboats.

As tradition expected, Captain Schoofs was the last to leave, and was picked up by a boat from the *Ford Castle*. As dawn rose, a lifeboat from the *Achilles* rowed to where men were still struggling in the water: all were rescued and were later landed at Cherbourg, Schoofs had to wear a Dutch officer's uniform loaned by the Captain of the *Achilles*.

One person died while trying to escape the liner. This was an engineering officer, Jaureguy, but whether he struck the hull on the way down or hit wreckage in the water was never determined.

Later records established that *Achilles* rescued 34, the *Erato* 85, the *Ford Castle* 6 and the *Ruhr* 86, a total of 211. There was some confusion about the presence of women on board. A contemporary article in *L'Illustration* and various local, national and international newspapers and magazines reported on three, some even publishing a photograph with their names and apparent jobs, but later company reports strenuously denied this.

Manicurist Miss Jacques, masseuse Miss Champagnat and saleswomen Miss Dolora.

With no more survivors on board the burning hulk, the rescue ships headed for Cherbourg. First to arrive at the quayside was *Achilles*, at 4pm. Dressed mostly in clothes supplied by the crews of the rescuing ships, and having lost all of their personal possessions, the survivors were sent to the Hôtel Atlantique, cheap basic accommodation usually used for emigrants leaving the country. Here they were given fresh clothing, warm food and allowed to sleep.

The French Navy, alerted by the authorities at Cherbourg, had instructed Captain Mailloux, in the minesweeper *Pollux*, to head for the scene. *Pollux* was a converted Russian icebreaker of 2,400 tons.

Sud Atlantique's representative at Cherbourg, Camille Quoniam, and M. Le Rouge, head of maritime affairs at the port, were also alerted. Vice Admiral Le Dô, in charge of the maritime police at the port, ordered two naval tugs, *Barfleur* and *Ramier*, to leave immediately. Next the Vice Admiral requested two seaplanes from the Chantereyne base fly over the scene and bring back eyewitness reports. Captain Dros and Lieutenant Legendre returned in the early afternoon, reporting that the liner was drifting, and surrounded by a thick pall of black smoke, with a list of at least 15 degrees, although there didn't seem to be any more flames. Several boats were in the vicinity. Soon after the Admiral sent another two seaplanes, requesting more detail. The pilots returned, confirming the earlier reports and stressing the extent of damage that they had seen.

By 3pm *Pollux* arrived at the scene, some 22 miles off the Casquets. An English destroyer, *Westcott*, was there; as soon as the French vessel appeared they exchanged courtesies and the destroyer left. Several English planes were circling. Captain Mailloux's first job was to slowly circle the wreck, studying everything in case there were any more survivors on board. The Vice Admiral had ordered that if *L'Atlantique* became a danger to navigation for other ships, Mailloux was to sink the hulk immediately. He ordered Mailloux to prevent anyone other than a French salvage crew getting on board, to preserve salvage rights.

Top: *Rescue tugs arrive.*   Right: *Survivors on a rescue vessel.*

Rotterdam then reported: "French steamer *L'Atlantique*, reported on fire in Channel: Messrs. L. Smit & Co., Rotterdam and Maassluis, sent tug *Roode Zee* from Falmouth, *Lauwerzee* from Brest, and *Witte Zee* from Hook of Holland."

From Berlin, Reuters reported: "The Hamburg-Amerika Line has received a wireless from the motor vessel *Ruhr* stating that the latter has taken aboard 80 of the crew of the liner *L'Atlantique*."

Reuters in Paris issued the first detailed report of the disaster: It was 4 o'clock this morning that the first SOS from the *L'Atlantique* was picked up by the German motor vessel *Ruhr* and the British steamer *Ford Castle*. Both rushed at full speed to the rescue, the *Ruhr* arriving first. The sea was rough, the weather thick and drizzly, but the liner stood out in the dusk like a flaming beacon."

St Catherine's Point reported the following messages received from Niton Wireless Station: (from Ford Castle at 1.00pm) "Rescued chief officer and four of crew from burning *L'Atlantique*. Lost port lifeboat. Landing them at Cherbourg."

(from Highland Chieftain at 2.02pm) "*L'Atlantique* 20 miles west of Casquets burning fiercely fore and aft, listing heavily to port, danger to navigation. Received signal from steamer *Sierra Salvada* nobody remaining on board. Have examined burning vessel at close quarters no sign of life, consider impossible for anyone to survive longer on board owing heat and smoke. Have no survivors on board *Highland Chieftain*, now proceeding London."

The Salvage Association in London received the following message
from Messrs. L. Smit & Co., Rotterdam dispatched 3.46pm:
"Steamer L'Atlantique totally abandoned burning fore to aft, heavy
list to port, prospects of keeping afloat considered poor."

Reuters gave more detail: "A French seaplane with two officers who
have flown over the burning liner have made the following report
to the Maritime Prefect: 'The L'Atlantique is in a very bad position
and the fire is raging in both the fore and aft quarters of the vessel,
which already has a list of 20 degrees. No flames are visible, but
only a thick smoke which obscured the view of the aviators. The
rescue ships, including the Ruhr and the Dutch steamer Achilles are
grouped around the liner without being able to approach her. For the
moment no attempt at extinguishing the flames is possible."

On Thursday 5 January many of the national papers in the UK,
Europe and America were carrying the story. A typical report in *The
Times* declared:

FRENCH LINER ON FIRE: Feared loss of life, burning all day
Captain's story
A fire which broke out early yesterday in the French liner *L'Atlantique*,
while she was in the Channel on her way to Le Havre, has practically
gutted the ship. Up to a late hour the fire was still burning, and with
a freshening of the wind the sea had become rather rough.

There were no passengers aboard, but *L'Atlantique* carried a crew of
about 230. The great majority were taken off by other steamers, and
211 were landed at Cherbourg. It is feared that 17 or 18 men have
been lost. *L'Atlantique*, which was a luxury liner of over 40,000 tons,
was insured for sums amounting to about £2,000,000 at present rates
of exchange, for the greater part in the London market.

The Times' *Paris correspondent reported in the same edition:*
The liner *L'Atlantique*, of 42,500 tons gross, belonging to the French
Sud Atlantique Company, which runs an express passenger service
from Bordeaux to South America, caught fire west of the Channel
Islands this morning when on her way from Bordeaux to Le Havre.

The fire spread rapidly, and in spite of the efforts of the ship's crew was
soon out of control. The crew abandoned ship and were picked up by
other vessels. It is feared that 17 or 18 of them have perished. Messages
from Cherbourg suggest that a number of them were injured.

At the time of writing it was reported that the ship was a total loss,
though she had not sunk. Tugs and salvage vessels from Cherbourg
had arrived near the wreck, but were unable to approach it owing to
the great heat and dense clouds of smoke.

FIRST MESSAGE
L'Atlantique was being taken to Le Havre for dry docking and
repairs. She carried about 230 men. The first intimation of
the disaster was received at the naval headquarters at Brest and
Cherbourg at 8.30am. It said: 'French liner *L'Atlantique* is on fire at
49deg 30 North, 3deg 17 West. Steamer *Ruhr* is on the scene and
has taken the crew on board.'

Drifting and abandoned. Lifeboat 15 can be seen dangling down the side of the hull, still suspended from one of the falls.

SURVIVORS LANDED AT CHERBOURG
Captain's Account of Disaster

Most of the survivors from *L'Atlantique* were landed at Cherbourg this afternoon. Among them was the captain, who had remained in his ship until the last possible moment and then jumped into the sea.

Captain Schoofs said after landing that the fire began early this morning, when *L'Atlantique* was approaching the Channel Islands. At 3.30am the night watchman reported to him that a first class cabin was on fire. The alarm was sounded and the fire-fighting appliances of the ship were brought into action.

At first the officers thought it would be possible to extinguish the fire without calling for assistance. But it spread very rapidly owing to the large areas of paint and varnish in the cabins, and after two or three hours it was seen to be out of control.

L'Atlantique then tried to call for help, but her wireless station was full of smoke and the operator was half asphyxiated. Only one faint and mutilated signal sent out by him was received on shore. The first effective call for help was eventually sent out by the German steamer *Ruhr* at 8.30.

Meanwhile the captain had given the order to abandon ship at 6am. The crew were then at their boat stations, and the boats were lowered. The *Ruhr* also lowered her boats. One of the large lifeboats of the *L'Atlantique* capsized when lowered owing to the breaking of the falls, and its occupants were thrown into the water. Some of them were picked up, but the rest were drowned. The captain also feared that a few men had been trapped by the flames or made unconscious by the smoke on board the ship.

L'Atlantique left Bordeaux with about 230 men on board. The British steamer *Ford Castle* landed six survivors at Cherbourg this afternoon; the *Achilles* landed 33, including two slightly injured; the *Ruhr* landed 80. The Dutch vessel *Erado*, which had intended to make for Brest with another 84 survivors, changed her route and landed them at Cherbourg this evening.

At the time of telegraphing *L'Atlantique* was still afloat and within a few miles of the scene of the outbreak of fire. She was still burning, and was wrapped in a dense cloud of smoke, which made it impossible to approach her. All the internal fittings and superstructure had been destroyed, and the ship was reduced to a hulk of twisted metal.

Another detailed report was carried in Lloyd's List that day:

GREAT LINER ON FIRE IN CHANNEL

The French South American liner *L'Atlantique*, the twelfth largest vessel afloat, caught fire in the Channel yesterday morning and was subsequently abandoned by her crew. According to the latest news received last night she had a list of 20 degrees, and the heat was so intense that the vessels in the vicinity were unable to do anything. A telegram from Lloyd's Agent at Havre stated that the vessel was totally on fire bows to stern. A communiqué issued by the French Ministry of Mercantile Marine stated that the vessel might be regarded as lost. It was hoped that the entire crew had been saved. It is understood the M. Leon Meyer, the Minister of Mercantile Marine, has proceeded to Cherbourg with officials of the Ministry in order to conduct an inquiry into the disaster.

RESCUE OF THE CREW

Messages received at Lloyd's from agents and wireless stations gave the position of *L'Atlantique* as lat. 40°30′N, long. 3°17′W, or about 20 miles west of Guernsey. She was carrying a crew of only about 260 and no passengers. A wireless message from the liner *Highland Chieftain*, received at 2.2pm, stated that *L'Atlantique* was burning fiercely fore and aft and was listing heavily to port; a close examination of the vessel showed no sign of life on board. Eighty of the crew were picked up by the German motorship *Ruhr* and five by the British steamer *Ford*

Castle. Many tugs, salvage craft and other vessels hastened to the spot, but for some hours were unable to assist.

INSURANCES ON THE SHIP

A correspondent writes: On first news of the casualty 60 guineas per cent. was quoted on *L'Atlantique*, the rate rising to 80 guineas on a report that she had been abandoned, and falling again to 65 guineas when this report was contradicted by a news agency. When, however, it was definitely reported that she had been abandoned, was burning fiercely fore and aft, and listing heavily, she became uninsurable, after the rate had risen again to 80 guineas per cent.

The insurances on the vessel are effected on a value of 100,000,000f (approximately £1,176,500 at current exchange), while supplementary insurances on "total loss only" risks being the total covered on hull interests to about £2,000,000, of which approximately £1,250,000 is understood to be covered in the London market. Even at £2,000,000 the vessel would appear to be underinsured, however, for when building at the Chantiers et Ateliers de St Nazaire, Penhoët, she was insured for approximately £2,900,000, and when completed was estimated to have cost at least £3,000,000. It is understood that her present insurances are effected on French policy conditions, under which the assured has the right to tender abandonment if the cost of repairs amounts to 75 per cent of the insured value, in which case a "constructive total loss" becomes payable.

The next report from Havre on Reuters stated: "The steamer *Achilles*, with the crew of the steamer *L'Atlantique* on board, is expected to reach here at 8pm. It is believed that there are injured among the crew of the *L'Atlantique*, and hospital equipment is expected to reach here at about 8pm. Five 'planes have left Le Bourget to make a report on the situation. Captain Dros, who is in command of the aeroplane base at Chantereyne and has just returned from a flight over the burning liner, is going out again to make a further report. The Cherbourg representative of the Compagnie de Navigation Sud Atlantique has left in a tug to meet the crew of the liner.

L Smit Rotterdam reported: Tug *Roode Zee* reached steamer at 3.30pm on 5 Jan, position lat 49.51N, long 2.38W, on fire from fore to aft, impossible connect at present, wind WSW, gentle breeze.

A Reuters report later on 4 January from Cherbourg:

A dramatic narrative of the disaster to the liner *L'Atlantique* was given tonight by Captain Schoofs, her commander, who was among the 211 rescued landed here. He says he believes that 30 members of the crew perished but official figures indicate that there are only 18 missing. The master was the last to leave the ship, jumping into the sea. He was picked up by the Dutch steamer *Achilles*.

"We were off Guernsey at 3.30 this morning," Captain Schoofs said, "when it was reported that a fire had broken out in a first-class cabin. We lost no time in trying to master the outbreak. I thought we had succeeded in doing so, but we were beaten by the very inflammable varnish, which acted like a fuel to the fire, and the flames spread along the electric cables from cabin to cabin. Soon the whole first-class accommodation was ablaze.

The wireless operator tried to give the alarm but his room was almost immediately a mass of flame and smoke. He managed to send out one SOS, which was picked up feebly by Bleville, near Havre. Then he had to make his escape.

At 6 o'clock we had to abandon all hope of saving the ship. I ordered the crew to take to the boats. Unfortunately in one case the hawser broke or was burned and the boat overturned, throwing the occupants into the sea. Other members of the crew were penned up in the boiler-room, where they died of suffocation."

A later report from Reuters added the following:

The Minister of Merchant Marine arived here late last night for the purpose of opening an inquiry into the cause of the disaster. He immediately visited the survivors at the Hotel des Emigrants. He then held a conference with the Marine Authorities and with Captain Schoofs of the ill-fated vessel. Afterwards, in an interview, he declared that the cause of the outbreak of the fire remained uncertain. The most striking fact that had emerged, he said, was the extraordinarily short space of time that elapsed after the outbreak before the conflagration assumed catastrophic proportions. It had soon become apparent that it would be impossible to cope with the flames. Captain Schoofs declared that he still entertained some hopes of towing in the derelict liner, and that he was deterined to attempt the task. He admitted, however, that it would be certain to prove a very difficult one to accomplish. The number of persons believed to be still missing from *L'Atlantique* remains at 17. Out of the 226 who left Bordeaux in the vessel 211 have been accounted for. Twenty-seven of them are injured, most of them slightly. Two doctors and an officer, however, are badly burned. A number of those who were rescued were women. The Dutch steamer *Erato* is the last to have brought in survivors, and she has landed 84 men, which, with the total of 127 landed from the other vessels, makes in all 211. The British steamer *Ford Castle*, the German motor vessel *Ruhr* and the Dutch steamer *Achilles* left Cherbourg as soon as they had landed the survivors whom they had picked up.

That night the wind increased from the south-south-west. The hulk started to drift with the effect of the wind and tide towards the English coast, near Portland Bill.

Several salvage companies kept powerful tugs in ports along the English Channel – French, Dutch, German and English. They were all aware of the disaster, and were anxious to be involved in the race for the salvage rights of such a valuable vessel.

A French tug, the *Abeille XXII*, was in the English Channel. Three other French tugs from the same company, the *Abeille XXI, Abeille XXIV* and *Abeille XXVI* prepared to leave Le Havre. Another French tug, the *Minotaure* owned by the CGT, prepared to leave Brest under Captain le Friant. She had special firefighting equipment aboard as well as being an extremely powerful towing vessel. Also in Brest was another French

Captain Schoofs in earnest discussions with Minister Léon Meyer.

salvage vessel, the *Iroise*, a converted Russian icebreaker, and a Dutch tug, the *Lauwerzee*, under Captain Van Dyck.

Two other Dutch tugs joined in: the *Roodezee* under Captain Klinge, came from Falmouth, and the *Wittezee* came from Folkestone. A German tug, the *Simson*, under Captain Reinecke, left Flessingue.

By 11.30pm *Minotaure* arrived at the scene, with the others arriving through the night. Although the hulk was drifting, there was no obvious danger to shipping at that point: Captain Mailloux ordered the two French naval tugs, the *Ramier* and the *Barfleur*, back to Cherbourg. The civilian tugs circled the wreck to assess the dangers; the heat and smoke were too intense for any close approach, or to make any salvage attempts. Most present were still convinced that as the fire continued, the liner would simply roll over and sink sooner or later. The list was increasing, and plates were buckling.

Niton Wireless station reported: Tug *Lauwerzee* signalled 4.49am today at burning *L'Atlantique* off Guernsey.

The Salvage Association received the following message from Messrs. L. Smit & Co., dispatched from Rotterdam 7am today, the message being received from their tug *Roode Zee* in the vicinity of the vessel: *L'Atlantique* now S of Portland, no fire, heavy smoking only. Weather moderating SSW to W. Ship listing to port. Several French tugs here. Vessel not yet approachable.

St Catherine's Point reported a message received from Niton Radio: From Dutch tug *Roode Zee* at 9.35am: *L'Atlantique* drifting north 136 degrees, true, distant eight miles from Portland Lighthouse.

Reuters next report stated: The burnt-out shell of the French liner *L'Atlantique* is now rapidly drifting towards the English Coast. The Maritime Prefecture here states that from the direction in which she is making she will probably run aground somewhere between Portland and the Isle of Wight.

A special vessel has been dispatched to follow her as she nears the English Coast in order to safeguard shipping in case the weather should be foggy. The latest news of *L'Atlantique* comes from the minelayer *Pollux* which saw her drifting in a northerly direction with a strong wind behind her.

The minesweeper reported that the fire appeared to have abated somewhat, though flames could still be seen at the bows and the stern. Five tugs have set out to try to tow the hull back to Cherbourg.

Reuters reported: Captain Schoofs is to leave Cherbourg on board the tug *Ramier*, which will rush him towards *L'Atlantique*. This decision has been taken with the consent of M. Beter, a director of the Cie. Sud Atlantique, the owners, who is anxious that a French vessel shall follow the wreck in order to be on the spot as soon as it is possible to come near to it.

Meanwhile the steamer *L'Atlantique* has a much greater list than was noticeable yesterday, and seems to have sprung a leak in the stern, since clouds of steam are to be seen mingling with the smoke from the flames.

The inquiry into the cause of the disaster has now opened in the Hôtel des Emigrants at Cherbourg. Both the men who gave the alarm, and those who took part in the attempt to extinguish the flames, are being closely interrogated. M Léon Meyer, the French Minister of Merchant Marine, is attending the proceedings.

The Salvage Association received a message from Messrs. L. Smit & Co.: Tugs *Roode Zee* and Simson connected with steamer *L'Atlantique* forward, French tugs connected aft same time. Nobody on board ship. Waiting for port of destination. The position given at the time was approximately 7 miles E of Portland.

The hull was still extremely hot, and sea and winds were still rough. All the salvage craft were anxious to secure their lines to the vessel before she ran aground, but they were not able to approach to get towlines aboard. The wind veered slightly: the liner started to drift away from the coast. Another naval tug, the *Mastodonte*, arrived at 9.53am, and by 10am the German tug *Simson* arrived from Hamburg.

Although the fire was now beginning to burn itself out, the hull was still too hot for the tugs to get close enough to begin salvage operations. In the meantime Captain Schoofs had met with the representatives from Sud Atlantique. He decided to return to *L'Atlantique*, with his chief officer and fifteen volunteers from the original crew, on board the naval tug *Ramier*.

Mailloux was advised by telegraph that Schoofs was returning, and that *Minotaure* was authorised by the company to handle the subsequent operations. *Pollux* attempted to transmit the information to *Minotaure*, without much success, and at 1.05pm passed the information across verbally.

The wind was lessening, and the smoking wreck was now six miles south of the Shambles. *Abeille XXIV* approached but failed to get its line aboard. *Roodezee* tried next, using a rocket launcher to fire a line aboard the bow of the liner.

Next *Iroise* moved in, but was blocked on two attempts by other tugs. *Simson* took over the other end of the tow line from the *Roodezee*; both tugs started to move forward but failed to move the liner against the effects of the tide.

Minotaure managed to attach its hawser to the stern anchor, with the help of a crewman who had scrambled up. Around 1.30pm *Minotaure* moved away, and *L'Atlantique* moved with her: she was finally under tow. Mailloux on *Pollux* was close by, watching the scene through his binoculars; he noted that by 1.45pm the liner was definitely moving under the effect of *Minotaure's* towline.

The towline between *Roodezee* and *Simson* was still not taut, and they were obviously having no effect. For the next few minutes *L'Atlantique* was clearly being towed by *Minotaure*, then the combined tow of *Roodezee* and *Simson* came into effect in the opposite direction, and the tow was stalemated. Mailloux approached both the *Roodezee* and *Simson* and informed them that they had begun towing ten minutes after *Minotaure*, but they each refused to accept this. While the discussion was going on, both *Abeille's* had managed to attach themselves at the stern, and were now adding to the tow.

from Lloyd's List & Shipping Gazette, *Friday 6 January*

L'Atlantique Adrift Off English Coast

The French South American liner *L'Atlantique*, which caught fire and was abandoned early on Wednesday, was adrift in the Channel for the greater part of yesterday, with a large number of tugs and other craft standing by. Apparently no attempt was made to board the vessel. Late in the afternoon the Salvage Association received a telegram from Messrs. L. Smit & Co., to the effect that the tugs *Roode Zee* and *Simson* had been able to make connection forward and at the same time French tugs connected aft, the position being given as approximately seven miles east of Portland. Nobody was on board. It was the tugowner's suggestion that in view of the direction of the wind and the distance, efforts should be made to tow *L'Atlantique* to Solent, and to fight the fire there. An inquiry into the cause of the disaster was opened in the Hôtel des Emigrants at Cherbourg yesterday. Some doubt still exists as to the exact loss of life. Official figures issued by the French Ministry of Marine on Wednesday night gave the number of officers and men on board as 229. Of these, 211 were landed at Cherbourg by the *Ruhr*, *Ford Castle*, *Achilles* and *Erato*. Several of the survivors were injured.

Captain's Narrative

Captain Schoofs, in an account of the fire given to Reuters, said the wireless operator's room was quickly enveloped and became a deathtrap, making it impossible to send out SOS messages. One of *L'Atlantique's* boats overturned as it was being lowered, resulting in loss of life. A number of men were caught like rats in a trap in the boiler room and died of suffocation. The captain was the last to leave the ship, jumping into the sea. He was picked up by the Dutch steamer *Achilles*.

Later it was reported that Captain Schoofs had left Cherbourg on board the tug *Ramier* for the blazing vessel. This decision was taken with the consent of M. Beter, a director of the Cie. Sud Atlantique, who is anxious that a French vessel shall follow the wreck in order to be on the spot as soon as it is possible to come near to it.

In addition to the Dutch tugs in attendance five tugs were reported to have left Cherbourg for the vessel, and also the mine-layer *Pollux*. The burning vessel was sighted from many points of the English coast yesterday between Portland Bill and the Needles. The weather was described as fairly calm, with wind SSW to W. The Portland coast-guard reported that he saw no flames at any time, but billowy clouds of smoke. The hull had a list of about 20 deg. Her foremast had gone, but the smoke seemed to be coming from the stern, not from the fore part of the vessel. She was still burning at midday. At that time tugs approached the vessel to pump water into her smoking stern. Most of the salvage craft were using their powerful air compressors to pump water into her, and the crews were working desperately to get the vessel under control while the calm weather lasted. The burning liner was visible shortly after 1pm, 12 miles south-west of St Alban's Head. She was surrounded by five or six tugs ans was slowly moving westward with the tide. Only a little smoke could be seen coming from the vessel. With the aid of glasses it could be made out that the bridge and the foremast were missing. At 3.45pm Lloyd's Signal Station at the Needles sighted the vessel, bearing south-west, approximately 18 miles distant. She was stated to be still on fire, and the vessel's list appeared to have increased. The weather was given as light westerly wind, barometer 30.08, rising, visibility good and sea slight.

From the London Times *of 6 January, by a special correspondent reporting from Portland:*

The appearance of *L'Atlantique* drifting off Portland this morning caused great excitement on the South coast.

She was sighted about 4 o'clock, but not at first recognized. From the coastguard station and from Portland Bill lighthouse the lights of craft accompanying her were seen, and a close watch was kept from both places.

At dawn the derelict liner became plainly visible. A strong south wind had brought her within about six miles of Portland, east of the Bill, and she was drifting dangerously towards the coast. She was still emitting smoke, which occasionally screened her from view, but there were periods when her hull could be distinctly seen. Her three funnels were standing, as well as her mainmast, but the foremast had gone. She was drifting with her stern towards the English coast. Her hull was about 30ft out of the water, and she had a considerable list.

News of the presence of the liner near Portland and Weymouth spread quickly on land, and the drifting liner was watched from many places on the coast. She was estimated at one time to have been within three miles of Portland Bill, drifting towards the shore, but a change of tide helped to stop her approach.

This was followed by a change of wind, which became north-westerly, and the liner drifted slowly in an easterly direction up the Channel. She was near the coast off Portland until about 1 o'clock.

With the aid of glasses she was followed until after 4 o'clock. As she drifted her hull turned around and her bows pointed towards Portland. Her position at that time suggested that she was drifting on a course which, if continued, would take her between Cherbourg and Havre. This evening she was reckoned to be about 12 miles south of St Alban's Head and going towards the French coast.

Also in the London Times, *6 January, from the Cherbourg correspondent:*

L'Atlantique in tow: watch on the English coast

Tugs which have taken the burning French liner *L'Atlantique* in tow are making for Le Havre.

Telegraphing late last night our Cherbourg correspondent said that at the then rate of progress they would reach the French coast in about 30 hours. The fate of the liner depended on the wind.

The Paris correspondent for The Times *reported on 5 January:*

The burning wreck of *L'Atlantique* drifted north-eastwards across the Channel during the night, and was within a few miles of the English coast, near Portland, early this morning. The French minelayer *Pollux* and five French tugs followed the liner, but for many hours were unable to get near her owing to the great heat of her hull and the clouds of smoke which still poured from it.

Soon after dawn the fire in the central part of the ship seemed to be dying down, but thick smoke was still coming from the poop and forecastle. In the afternoon the French ships succeeded in getting a line on board *L'Atlantique* and taking her in tow. At the moment of writing they were escorting her slowly across the Channel in the direction of Le Havre. She was towed by four French and two Dutch tugs. The sea, which was rough this morning, had moderated and it was hoped that the liner might be brought to port without further mishap.

Minister and Enquiry

M. Léon Meyer, the Minister of Merchant Marine, arrived at Cherbourg last night and immediately went to see the survivors. After congratulating them on their escape, and on their fine conduct during the disaster, M. Meyer ordered each of them to tell the whole truth when questioned by the Committee of Inquiry. "You must tell all you know," he said, "and all that you saw. If you know of any constructional defect or imperfection you must say so. You will remember that your statements, if they are truthful and precise, may

enable us to take measures which will prevent the repetition of such a catastrophe."

The place of origin of the fire is now known – it began in a first-class cabin – and it is becoming evident that it was due to some accidental cause such as an electrical short-circuit. The theory of foul play is widely put forward in the French press today, but is emphatically rejected by survivors from the ship.

One of the officers of *L'Atlantique* has suggested as a possible explanation that the violent movement of the ship in the rough sea may have caused the breaking of an electric cable. She was in ballast only, and rolled heavily in the Channel. It is certain that the fire, once started, spread with extraordinary rapidity owing to the inflammable nature of the ship's internal fittings and the lavish use of thin painted and varnished wood panelling in her decoration.

Crew's Gallantry

All reports show that the officers and crew of *L'Atlantique* behaved with great gallantry and fought their hardest to the last possible moment to save their ship. The First and Second Captains, with a handful of men, were at last trapped by the flames on the bridge, and the First Captain, seeing the men hesitate to jump overboard, shouted to them to follow him and leaped into smoke-filled space. In many cases men half overcome by fumes and smoke fought their way back along the corridors to rescue comrades. Some who had fought until the last moment escaped through cabin portholes.

Minotaure and Abeille 24 *move in on the hulk.*

The next report in Lloyd's List gave the following: The French liner *L'Atlantique*, which has been on fire since dawn yesterday, has drifted to within a few miles of the English coast today. When the mist lifted at an early hour coastguards and people living near Portland Bill could see the liner still blazing. A Press Association reporter, telephoning about midday from Weymouth, said: The burning liner is now about six miles off Portland Bill, not far from the Shambles light vessel. She can be seen plainly. She is surrounded by eight tugs and also by what appears to be a French torpedo boat. Seen from the shore it appears as if attempts are being made to get some sort of line on board the vessel, but up to the present they have not succeeded in doing so. The weather is fairly calm, and there is not much wind. The set of the tide should bring the vessel nearer the

English coast, somewhere between Weymouth Bay and St Alban's Head. Later the liner drifted to a position four miles SE of Portland Bill, three miles from the Shambles light vessel. She was broadside on to a heavy swell with a list to starboard and drifting eastwards. Her after mast had been burned off and her stern appeared to be sinking. The fire seemed to be in the after starboard side where clouds of black smoke poured out. The liner was at midday only two miles from the dreaded Portland Race.

At midday tugs approached the vessel to pump water into the smoking stern. Most of the salvage craft are using their powerful air compressors to pump water into her, and the crews are working desperately to get the vessel under control while the present calm weather lasts. The liner stands high out of the water, with a list to starboard of about twenty degrees. She is moving only very slowly.

Lloyd's next report on 5 January gave: The burning liner *L'Atlantique* was visible shortly after 1pm 12 miles SW of St Alban's Head, which is between Swanage and Lulworth. She was surrounded by five or six tugs and was slowly moving east with the tide. Only a little smoke could be seen coming from the vessel. With the aid of glasses it could be made out that the bridge and foremast were missing. The wind was SW, with a slight sea running. Early this afternoon tugs got hawsers on the liner and took her in tow.

The Weymouth correspondent for the Daily Mail watched as sunrise came up at Portland Bill: As the news spread excited watchers on shore came and saw billows of smoke pouring from the vessel high into the skies, and shimmering waves of heat arose around her from the glowing hull. British, French and Dutch tugs circled about her, their crews trying to get a line aboard and bring her under control. For six hours the heat and smoke held them at bay, and the *L'Atlantique*, uncontrolled and helpless, was until late in the afternoon a plaything of the tide, the north-west wind, and dangerous Channel currents.

Fears ran high near midday that the *L'Atlantique* would drift inside the Shambles bank, and on the the turning of the tide be borne aground somewhere on the Dorset shore. Almost imperceptibly however, she drifted away from Portland and out into the Channel.

Headlines in the *The Bournemouth Daily Echo* of Thursday 5 January declaimed: "Red hot hull now in tow – liner may be beached on the sands at Weymouth" The paper stated that, by that morning's edition, the hulk was in tow of tugs off the Dorset coast, and could be clearly seen from Portland, Lulworth and St Aldhelm's Head.

A further article was headlined:

Early morning surprise

When the mist lifted off the Dorset coast early this morning, coastguards and people living near Portland Bill were astonished to see the hulk of the French luxury liner, the *Atlantique*, which was ravaged by fire from stem to stern yesterday. She had drifted helplessly in the Channel, before a wind that drove her towards the English coast.

Abeille XXIV had come very close alongside, and Captain Pichard and radio officer Hébert scrambled on board. Mailloux noticed the Frenchmen at 2.45pm. Around this time another Dutch tugboat, *Lauwerzee*, arrived.

The *Iroise* again came in and managed to attach its line, but had come too close and hit the stern, breaking its line at the same time. While they were in close, Captain Nicolas threw a line to Hébert with the company's house flag; Hébert then managed to crawl to the stern, and raised the houseflag. It was now 3.40pm.

According to the Bournemouth Times: "An aircraft carrier, escorted by a destroyer in attendance, were passing through the Channel. The heavy mist meant several false reports were made confusing these two vessels for the *L'Atlantique* and a tug. Once the mist had lifted, *L'Atlantique* could be sighted from Anvil Point at 2.30pm, listing and drifting eastward, and later reported from Peveril Point. By 9.30pm she could be seen to be under tow, about 14 miles off the coast and apparently heading towards St. Catherine's. "

The Bournemouth Daily Echo reported: "At 11am *L'Atlantique* was between 6 and 7 miles off Portland Bill, and by noon had drifted within rather less than 2 miles off Shambles Bank."

The Swanage correspondent reported: "I estimate that the *L'Atlantique* is now around 12 miles off St. Aldhelm's Head and that she is drifting eastward at two miles an hour."

Two of the Abeille tugs close in on the stern.

By 4pm another Dutch tug had arrived, the *Witte Zee*; around the same time the French naval tug *Mastodonte* moved in and managed to retrieve the two men on the wreck. *Simson* released its tow, although *Roodezee* was still grimly hanging on; eventually she too had to give up the unequal struggle. One of the Dutch boats tried to get their men on board, but failed. The tugs were no longer having any effect on the liner – *L'Atlantique* had stopped. This immediately concerned Captain Mailloux, who signalled *Minotaure* that they must get moving again.

Sailors from the *Lauwerzee* were next to try to board the liner. Wygeree and de Baar succeeded, but the third, Van Teylingen, was climbing a burned rope, which gave way under his weight. He grabbed another rope before he fell into the sea, and the other two pulled him aboard. However, Mailloux had not seen them at that time.

Mailloux signalled *Minotaure* that it had the owner's authority for the salvage, and that it should not only resume the tow but should also try to come to an arrangement with the other vessels.

Signals passed between *Pollux, Minotaure* and several of the tugs, but they were either being misunderstood or incorrectly answered. Whether this was a deliberate attempt to stall for time or not was unclear, but while it was going on it appeared that *Lauwerzee* had slipped through and cut the tow lines of both *Abeille* tugs.

It was now 6.40pm, and *Ramier* arrived with Schoofs. Mailloux radioed a report of the situation to Schoofs, also advising him about the Dutchmen on board the wreck. Schoofs, with the volunteers, transferred to *Abeille XXIV*, and was then advised by Captain Le Friant of the various events of the last 24 hours.

Schoofs made it clear that he was in charge of salvage operations. However, the weather was adverse – during the night they had experienced strong winds, lightening and hail storms so Schoofs postponed any immediate attempt to board *L'Atlantique*.

Schoofs returned to take control.

A Reuters report from Cherbourg, filed late on 5 January: According to later messages from the minelayer *Pollux*, the tug *Ramier*, with Captain Schoofs of *L'Atlantique* on board, has come up with the convoy. It will not be possible for him to board *L'Atlantique* until tomorrow morning. The speed of the convoy is given as three knots and it is hoped that if the wind remains favourable to bring the vessel into Havre tomorrow evening.

Again the various tugboats started to manœuvre to gain precedence in any subsequent towing and salvage. The German tug *Simson* moved in on the port side and got a line aboard. Schoofs ordered them to let go, but they refused. Mailloux moved in with *Pollux* to repeat the order, but they still refused, so next Mailloux decided to try to cut their tow line. This failed, but in the attempt the minesweeper got dangerously close to the drifting hulk, and Mailloux had to make some emergency manœuvres to avoid it.

Schoofs decided that it was necessary to get a Frenchman aboard the *L'Atlantique*. One of the volunteer crew, Lieutenant Even, offered to go. The captain of the *Abeille XXIV* moved in as close as possible, and a seaman on the forecastle tried to grab a rope hanging down the side of *L'Atlantique*, using a boat hook.

After several unsuccessful tries, Schoofs called to the Dutchmen still aboard, who were watching, to help. They threw a line to Even, who started to climb. Tragically as he started the two vessels swung towards each other, and the lieutenant's leg was trapped and crushed between the two hulls. It later had to be amputated.

The tugs start to get the tow under control, with Roode Zee at the front.

During this time events were very confused, with various tugboats moving in and and backing off. The only impartial report covering the whole salvage operation was that later submitted by Captain Mailloux, which proved invaluable when claims and counterclaims were made.

In his report, Mailloux was adamant that *Simson* moved in and affixed a towline without first being authorised, leading to the events in which Lieut Even's leg was crushed.

Similarly both *Roode Zee* and *Lauwerzee* refused to follow orders, or to accept that *Minotaure* had the company's authority to control the operation. He was adamant that *Lauwerzee* cut the towline of *Abeille XXIV* on the evening of January 5. He felt that without the presence of the French naval vessels, serious fighting would have broken out between the various crews at several stages; however, he concluded that by the end all the tugboats worked together under very difficult and dangerous conditions.

The Lloyd's agent at Cherbourg reported: French steamer *L'Atlantique* in tow of four tugs, port of destination not known as yet but probably Cherbourg.

A report from the Needles at 5.50pm: French liner *L'Atlantique* sighted at 3.45pm bearing south west 18 miles approximately. *L'Atlantique* last seen 4.55pm bearing south west about 16 miles. List on vessel appeared to have increased; there were about six tugs visible in vicinity of vessel. Weather, light westerly wind, blue sky, bar. 30.08 rising, visibility good, sea slight.

A report on 5 January, this from Weymouth, attributed to the 'News Chronicle': With fire still raging in her stern and flames sprouting from her bows. *L'Atlantique* is tonight a charred hulk in the Channel. Tugs and salvage vessels of four nations – British, French, German and Dutch – are in attendance, and an effort is being made to tow her to Havre. At midnight after many hours of skilful manœuvring, she had been moved a distance of about 12 miles.

A Reuters report, filed early on 6 January from Paris: At 9am steamer *L'Atlantique* was reported to be 70 miles from Havre. She is expected to reach Havre during the night, but will not enter port until tomorrow morning. The towing of the liner is proving difficult. Captain Schoofs wirelessed the Sud Atlantique last night: "I am on board tug *Abeille No 24*. I have kept the *Roode Zee* with me because she is the only tug with a towline forward. The *Minotaure* will remain tonight with a towline aft without pulling. We shall go on board *L'Atlantique* tomorrow, when I hope to tow her forward with an Abeille tug and the *Mastodonte*. The vessel is still burning. The F deck does not seem to have burned, but water poured in all day through three broken portholes on the waterline. We are trying to reach the French coast."

A report from Paris at 1.30pm: Reports regarding the progress of the steamer *L'Atlantique* are somewhat conflicting. Cherbourg states that the convoy towing the burned liner to Havre is having to fight strong currents and has not advanced since 8 o'clock this morning. On the other hand, the Ministry of Mercantile Marine announce that the liner is now only 60 miles from Havre, an advance of 10 miles from the position at 9am. All the morning there was still some doubt whether *L'Atlantique* would after all be taken into Cherbourg, from which she was only 35 miles distant, but Reuter learned from Havre at 1.15pm that she was expected there late tonight.

Smit of Rotterdam reported: Roode Zee 12.15pm: Since last message *Simson* connected midnight. Heavy squall during night, *Witte Zee* parted 1.40am, connected again 8am forward, *Iroise* connected forward. Now towing under command of *Roode Zee, Witte Zee, Lauwerzee, Iroise, Abeille XXI* and *XXII. Minotaure* parted. Destination altered 11.15 to Cherbourg. Position 9.30am, lat.50.7N, long. 1.6W. Wind W by N, moderate breeze.

From Lloyd's List, Saturday 7 January:

Burning Liner Bound for Cherbourg: The Origin of the Fire

The burning French liner *L'Atlantique*, which had been drifting in the Channel all day Thursday, was taken in tow by several tugs on Thursday evening, and although little progress was made at first a message from the Dutch tug *Roode Zee*, dispatched at 12.15pm yesterday, stated that three Dutch and three French tugs were connected, and were towing the vessel towards Cherbourg. The lower hold was still burning. The position at 9.30am was lat. 50.7 N, long. 1.6 W.

Captain Schoofs arrived at Cherbourg yesterday in the *Abeille XXIV* with two injured men, one being the wireless operator, who was one of the first to go on board *L'Atlantique*. He sustained injuries to the chest in the course of the operations. The second man had his foot crushed when trying to board the liner. Captain Schoofs was returning to *L'Atlantique* at once.

The question, "How did the fire in *L'Atlantique* originate?" was to be raised at yesterday morning's Cabinet Council, at which M. Leon Meyer, Minister of Merchant Marine, was expected to state what he had been able to glean from the first inquiry, states Reuter. "I do not believe that the disaster was due to sabotage," he had already stated emphatically. "Only two hypotheses are permissible, either there was a short circuit, which seems unlikely as the electrical fittings of the vessel were in perfect order, or else the fire was due to the carelessness of a smoker. The fire originated in a cabin where 30 woollen mattresses were stored. One of the men who moved them there may well have let fall a spark and the mattress may have smouldered for days."

Discovery of the Fire

A graphic account of how the fire was discovered was given by a telephonist who, wakeful, went up to watch his comrade on duty. He watched a man sweeping a corridor. "What a dust you are making," he said, but he soon noticed that the dust was smoke coming from beneath the door of cabin 232, in which the mattresses were stored. When the door was opened a stifling cloud poured out. No doubt was possible and the alarm was given.

The following Reuter message was dispatched from Paris on Thursday night: The latest news of the injured members of *L'Atlantique*'s crew is that they are only four in number and that none of them is seriously hurt. They include the ship's doctor and the second officer.

A report by the Daily Telegraph, *covered in Lloyd's List, stated:*
With fires still burning in her in four places and smoke rising from her decks, steamer *L'Atlantique* arrived in Cherbourg Roads about 11 o'clock tonight. Tugs are now trying to manœuvre her into port in the darkness. It is considered that the damage to *L'Atlantique* is so severe that she can only be broken up for scrap when she gets into port. Seven tugs, three Dutch, three French and one German, made the tow at a rate of from two to three knots, with frequent stops.

It was intended to bring the liner to Havre, but threatening weather made it necessary to alter the course and make for Cherbourg. The set of the tide was making the vessel's list dangerous. The change of course lessened the danger. Despite the accident to Lieut. Evain [sic], Captain Schoofs, with a party of 15 volunteers, managed to get on board his vessel from one of the tugs this afternoon. Big gaps, showing the fire still raging below, were found in the upper decks. Captain Schoofs tried to descend to the lower decks, but the smoke and heat were too intense and he was beaten back every time. Later he returned to Cherbourg.

A question of salvage may be raised as a result of a singular incident during the tow. Tonight a French eye-witness informed me that the German tug (the *Simson*) was already attached to the liner by a cable when the commander of *L'Atlantique*, Captain Schoofs, asked the master of the tug to withdraw. This he refused to do, and the French mine layer *Pollux* made two unsuccessful attempts to cut the cable of the *Simson*.

No further attempt was made to carry out this manœuvre and the German tug continued to assist the French and Dutch tugs.

According to Lloyd's List of 7 January: The charred hulk of the liner *L'Atlantique* has been taken in tow by the powerful French tug *Minotaure* together with two other French tugs, a British tug and a Dutch tug, and is being brought to Havre, according to a message signalled by the minelayer *Pollux*.

Soon after this Havre announced: Steamer *L'Atlantique*, latest wireless information received states vessel will be towed to Cherbourg. *This was confirmed in messages from Cherbourg and from London.*

Cherbourg reported: Captain Schoofs has just arrived here on board the tug *Abeille No. 24*, together with two injured men. Captain Schoofs is at once returning to the burning liner.

The Times, Saturday 7 January, filed from Cherbourg earlier in the day

Arrival in Harbour at Cherbourg: a precarious tow

The burned French liner L'Atlantique was brought safely into harbour here this morning. She anchored in the inner road just before a quarter to 1. Tugs had brought her close to the Homet signalling station last night, after having been 14 miles off Barfleur in the afternoon, and as the weather was calm and the night clear it was decided to bring her into port at once. The taking in tow of the liner proved to be a task of the greatest difficulty and danger, and two volunteers who attempted to board her were injured. One, M. Hébert, wireless operator of the tug *Abeille*, injured his chest; the other, Lieutenant Evan [sic], one of the officers of *L'Atlantique*, had his leg badly crushed between the hull of the tug *Ramier* and the side of the liner. Both men were landed here yesterday afternoon and taken to hospital.

The first man to set foot on the burning vessel on Thursday was Captain Pichard, of the Abeille Salvage Company. He made over 100 casts with a hastily improvised rope ladder before the hooks caught on the stern. Then, clambering aboard, he hoisted the French ensign. He was followed by three members of the crew of a Dutch tug, and between them they managed to get towlines aboard. Captain Pichard afterwards left the ship, but it appears the Dutchmen were unable to get away, and are still on board. It was not until yesterday morning that a sufficient number of hawsers were got on board to make the towing anything but a precarious process.

On 8 January, Niton Wireless Station reported: "Following received from British steamer *Stuart Star* at 12.25pm, GMT, passed alongside empty lifeboat, painted white, marked 20, believed to belong steamer *L'Atlantique*, position approximately lat. 50.9N, 1.24W."

Niton Wireless Station: Following received from Dutch steamer *Stad Zwoller* at 3.24pm: Open lifeboat No 23 of steamer *L'Atlantique*, of Bordeaux, drifting in lat. 53N, long. 2.17W, without crew; dangerous to navigation.

Reuters later reported: Steamer *L'Atlantique* arrived in the outer roads here shortly after 11pm. Tugs at once began manœuvring in an attempt to bring the hulk into the port. *The next report stated:* Steamer *L'Atlantique* was anchored in the inner roads at 12.40am.

In the same issue of The Times, *from the Paris correspondent:*

COMING INQUIRY
Minister of Justice to be consulted

At today's meeting of the Cabinet, M. Meyer, the Minister of Mercantile Marine, who had just returned from Le Havre, informed his colleagues of the results of the preliminary inquiry he had made there among the officers and crew into the causes of the outbreak of fire in *L'Atlantique*.

It is understood that M. Meyer attaches no importance to the suggestion that the ship was deliberately set on fire, and thinks it far more likely that the cause might be found in a short circuit or an act of sheer carelessness. On the other hand, the contractors have stated that the electrical wiring and fittings were carefully examined before the vessel left port.

M. Meyer, in a statement to the Press, said that the inquiry to be held in connexion with the fire in *L'Atlantique* would have to be something more than the customary technical investigation by a commission, and would be rather of a judicial character. The composition of the commission and its terms of reference would not be settled till he had conferred with the Minister of Justice.

On January 8, The New York Times continued this sad saga. 'The captains of the French, Dutch and German tugs which towed the burning liner *L'Atlantique* into Cherbourg tonight filed reports with the Chamber of Commerce there as a basis for settling the international controversy over claims for salvaging the French vessel. All are entitled to compensation.

If it is determined that *L'Atlantique* was abandoned, however, then the first tug to undertake salvage operations can claim a larger percentage of the prize money. It also remains to be settled whether the salvaged hulk now belongs to the Compagnie de Navigation Sud Atlantique or to the insurance companies.

Captain Schoofs contends his ship was never abandoned because when he went ashore, he invested the captain of the French tug *Minotaure* with authority to superintend the salvage operations. He charges that the Dutch and German tug captains later refused to obey, or at least ignored his orders. The French press generally deplores that the gallant work of saving the stricken liner should have given rise to a bitter fight amongst salvagers.

Reuters next report gave more details: As the sun rose this morning smoke could still be seen mounting steadily from the well deck and the poop of the steamer *L'Atlantique*, and there was a strong smell of burning oil. A few figures were observed on the upper deck making ready for the Cherbourg Harbour Fire Brigade, in a tug drawn up on the port side. If the firemen succeed in extinguishing the fire *L'Atlantique* will be brought into dry dock late this evening or tomorrow, but if it is not found feasible she may be beached on the bottom of the Eastern Harbour.

Rumours of trouble between the tugs towing the still smouldering hulk across the Channel have been reaching Cherbourg. At present all parties are reticent pending the filing of claims for whatever prize money may be available. Nevertheless, there is a rumour circulating among the seamen on the harbour side that the hawser connecting one tug to *L'Atlantique* was cut deliberately, and that another tug was rammed. At least one tug of non-French nationality has a decided list where she rests at anchor in the harbour.

Soon after, it was reported: Captain Trefie, of the tug *Iroise*, stated today: At 2.45pm on Thursday (Jan 5) we succeeded in getting a hawser fixed to *L'Atlantique*, but our stern was dashed against *L'Atlantique*, causing a huge dent. Then the hawser snapped. On Friday, at 8.30am, I crept in between the towlines of the tugs *Witte Zee* and *Simson*, and in spite of the heavy seas I came right up alongside *L'Atlantique* and manœuvred to pass a hawser over the port bow. We succeeded in this, but the hawser of the *Witte Zee* ran over our starboard bitts. In an endeavour to rid ourselves of the hawser we crept almost along its entire length up to the *Witte Zee*. But we could not get it overboard, and to avoid ramming her stern we were forced to cut the hawser of the *Witte Zee*. We had our hawser fixed at 10am, and with the weather improving all the time we were in Cherbourg at 11.40am last night. The master of the Dutch tug *Roode Zee* denied any suggestion of foul play to secure the wreck.

On Sunday, Cherbourg stated: Because of the danger threatened by the weather, the steamer *L'Atlantique* has been towed to a new position in deeper water opposite the Gare Maritime. Five bodies, two of which have been identified, have been found up to the present on board.

The Times, *Monday 9 January, from their correspondent at Cherbourg:*

French liner disaster: Bodies recovered from hull
Fires still burning

The burnt French liner *L'Atlantique*, which was anchored in the roadstead there during Friday night, was taken into dock yesterday evening. Two fires are still burning in her today.

The remains of five bodies have been found in the ship. The steamer *Solfurno* picked up one of her boats in the Channel this afternoon. The boat was empty. A technical committee is now engaged in examining the wreck of *L'Atlantique*.

Yesterday evening the wind had freshened so much that she threatened to break adrift and become a peril to shipping in the roadstead or block the harbour. The commander in chief, Admiral Le Dô, therefore gave orders for the ship to be brought into the only dock that would take her, which is the new deep-water dock alongside the uncompleted Marine Station. The docking was carried out in spite of protests from the port engineers and other authorities, who feared that the liner might sink in the new basin, or that her fuel oil might catch fire.

L'Atlantique's foremast has fallen and hangs over the ship's side almost touching the water, her funnels are awry, and her superstructure is twisted and blackened. The plates of her hull have 'rippled' owing to their expansion by heat. Nearly all the black paint which covered the hull has gone, leaving the red lead priming exposed, with the

Above: *Dutch tugs moored up.*
Right: *Roode Zee.*

As an interesting side issue, Captain Trifol of the *Abeille XXII* had originally taken *L'Atlantique* in tow after her launching.

The morning after the hulk arrived, ambulances and fire-engines stood by at the quayside. Five bodies had already been brought ashore.

Writer and politician John Baker White, a long-time opponent of both Nazis and Communists, was often called to investigate incidents

innumerable hieroglyphics of the builders still faintly visible. The ship's boats, which are of metal, lie as her crew left them. The one which capsized and threw its crew into the water still hung yesterday morning alongside the ship.

Staterooms gutted

The superstructure, saloons and staterooms, with their elaborate decorative fittings, are gutted. The bridge and charthouse, reduced to twisted sheets of metal, have bent backwards and collapsed. The roofs of the saloons and deckhouses have fallen to the deck below. There is not a scrap of woodwork left anywhere. Painted frescoes have melted and run down the walls, making pools of mixed colour. Lumps of melted pewter, copper and silver lie among fragments of scorched china in the pantries and dining rooms.

In the course of the salvage collisions occurred between the tugs themselves and between them and *L'Atlantique*. All the tugs bear traces of the collisions. The *Abeille 24* was dismasted. The *Abeille 22* had her rail ripped off. The *Iroise* had her stern bulwarks stove in when she was hurled against the liner. One tug cut another's hawser because it was under her keel, and threatened to foul her propeller. Another tug cut a hawser because it got in her tow bitts and threatened to force the tug between two others.

Lieutenant Even, of *L'Atlantique*, who had his foot crushed between a tug and the liner in trying to board her, had his foot amputated yesterday. He has been awarded the Order of Merit at Sea. A seaman who was slightly injured in the same way is progressing favourably.

Machinery undamaged

The examination of *L'Atlantique* and preparation for taking her into dry dock began this morning. Her machinery was found almost undamaged. One of her boilers was brought into action, and her own pump began to eject the water which had found its way into her. Before dark she lay on a more even keel.

Two identified bodies and other human remains found in the ship last night were put in coffins and boxes this afternoon and hoisted ashore. A short religious service was held over them in the station. The bodies were found in the lower part of the ship, and were those of men who had deliberately sacrificed themselves to keep the pumps going. Five pumps in the engine-room were kept at work until the end.

Of the fires still burning in the ship today one is forward and the other aft. The dock firemen passed their hoses through the scuttles to play water on them. The hull still had two hot spots, low down on either side near the stern, which made the water boil in the dock. These hot spots marked the position of the ship's refrigerator plant: the non-conducting material of the refrigerator, once thoroughly heated, held the heat for a long time.

Left: Survivors and some of the injured on the quayside.

of possible sabotage. He talked to many people that day. Members of the crew were emphatic that two fires had broken out almost simultaneously, both in cabins but on opposite sides of the ship. Closing the fire-proof doors should have limited the fire to one side of the ship.

Lloyd's List Tuesday 10 January: Cherbourg, Reuter 8 January: The fire is not yet extinguished, and according to the latest reports is still burning in two different parts fore and aft of the vessel. It is hoped, however, that it will be possible to bring her into dry dock on Tuesday 10 Jan. As a result of continual pumping the vessel's list has now been overcome and she rests again on an even keel. The committee of experts appointed by the Minister of Mercantile Marine to investigate the disaster started work here today examining the wreck and receiving the reports of the commanders of the various tugs who took part in the salvage work. The German commander (of the tug *Simson*) explained that the reason why he did not obey the orders of the French tug *Minotaure* and the minelayer *Pollux* was that he was acting under the orders of the Dutch tug *Roode Zee*, who was alone qualified to give him instructions. He also stated that the *Pollux* broke one of his hawsers and damaged another.

Lloyd's Report on Monday 9 January

L'Atlantique in port: moored in Cherbourg harbour

The French liner *L'Atlantique,* which was abandoned on fire on Wednesday, was towed into Cherbourg late on Friday and anchored in the inner roads at 12.30am Saturday. Later, because of the danger threatened by the weather, the vessel was towed to a new position in deeper water opposite the Gare Maritime.

According to a message from L Smit & Co, the vessel reached Cherbourg in tow of the Dutch tugs *Roode Zee, Witte Zee* and *Lauwerzee,* three French tugs and one German tug. The vessel then was still burning. Reuter reports that it is intended to place the vessel in dry dock as soon as events allow in the next few days. Five bodies, two of which have been identified, have been found on board. It is feared that the vessel's engines are entirely wrecked.

A Reuter message despatched from Cherbourg on Saturday states that rumours have been circulating that the hawser connecting one tug to *L'Atlantique* was cut deliberately, and that another tug was rammed. At least one tug of non-French nationality had a decided list where she anchored in the harbour.

Captain Trefie, of the French tug *Iroise* denied strongly the stories told on shore of unpleasant incidents between the Dutch and French boats in their efforts to be alone in the capture of the prize. "All nine tugs worked in perfect accord," he said. "We cut the hawser which fouled us at the last possible moment and prevented a worse disaster. From what I saw of the other incidents they were similar." The master of the Dutch tug *Roode Zee* denied any suggestion of foul play to secure the wreck.

The Committee of Experts appointed by the Minister of Merchant Marine proceeded to Cherbourg on Saturday evening to investigate the cause of the fire. It is anticipated that they will report very soon, with a view to enabling the Minister to draft a scheme of preventive measures.

The Minister has given orders that nobody shall be permitted to board *L'Atlantique* except the Committee. The eleven experts are composed of four representatives of the Ministry of Mercantile Marine, Colonel Pouderoux, commanding the Paris Fire Brigade, two electricians, three naval experts and one police commissioner.

New York Times, 8 January:
The Cherbourg maritime fire brigade today finally extinguished the last fire aboard *L'Atlantique*. It will not be until considerable work has been done, pumping out the hull and clearing up the wreckage, that an accurate estimate can be made of the value of what remains. If the ship is only good for scrap iron, it will bring $80,000 to $120,000. If, as is more likely, she can be reconditioned, she will be worth from $2,500,000 to $3,000,000. It was also rumoured tonight that several waiters and other workers had secretly boarded the ship at Bordeaux to obtain transportation to Le Havre and may have perished.

That morning Baker White had met Fred Memory, an experienced journalist for the UK *Daily Star* newspaper. Memory had already expressed concern over the SOS signals – or the absence of them – and advised Baker that he was to meet Captain Schoofs and the wireless operator. In the evening the two men met up to exchange information. Memory implied that Captain Schoofs felt at that time that the fire was the result of sabotage. This impression was later confirmed by another journalist, George Martelli, the Paris correspondent of the *Morning Post*, who had also interviewed Captain Schoofs.

Both journalists also confirmed something else. On board *L'Atlantique*, as on most ships, as the night watchmen patrolled the ship, they logged their movements on a small hand-held controller. This device was known to be with the purser, Muret, when he had arrived at Cherbourg, but since then both Muret and the watch controller had disappeared. Some days later Muret reappeared, claiming he had been to Paris to see the directors of Sud Atlantique, and that he had been acting under company instructions. Soon after this Muret was given a much-improved job on the Marseilles-Dakar run.

Another curious fact discovered by Memory was a conflict over the time the fire broke out. The sweeper Ferrugia said it was 3.45am, the telephonist Aramandia [or Raimandia?] claimed 4am. Only 15 minutes difference but it could be significant.

Once Baker had finished reading though Fred Memory's notes, he reminded him about his earlier comments regarding the SOS signals. The answer was very disturbing: "I cannot find a single piece of evidence to show that an SOS message was sent out at all, or if it was that anyone picked it up, although *L'Atlantique* had one of the most up-to-date wireless installations in the world."

Later enquiries showed that the earliest Brest heard a message was 6am, from the *Ruhr*. This message gave an interesting sequence of events:

5.30am L'Atlantique passed within 3/4 miles doing about 18 knots
6.10am Ascertained L'Atlantique stopped and on fire
6.20am Stations manned. Burning ship sighted
6.31am Ship called repeatedly. No reply
6.34am Niton (Isle of Wight) called. They had heard nothing
7.00am First boat-load picked up

Even though the Captain knew the fire was under the wireless room, it seemed obvious that an SOS had not been sent. At the Court of Inquiry, Captain Schoofs stated that "one feeble SOS" had been picked up at Le Havre. The wireless operator, Paul Creach from Bordeaux, was equally definite: he did not send out any SOS messages at the time in question. He had remained in the wireless room until 5.45am when he left briefly to visit an adjacent toilet. On his way back he received an order to send an SOS message, but by now the wireless room was full of smoke and he was unable to enter it. So for at least two hours after the fire had been discovered, it would appear that no signals were sent.

A colleague of Baker, Jim Finney, had gone to Bordeaux to see if anything unusual had happened before *L'Atlantique* left on her last voyage. He learnt that when *L'Atlantique* had left for her last trip to South America, she had grounded on a sand bank at Pauillac. The harbour master sent divers to examine the hull: they found that several plates were buckled, but stated that the liner was still seaworthy. The harbour master sent his report to the Ministry of Marine, as he was required to do for such incidents. However, no copy of the report into this incident could be found. This would have been invaluable to the insurers and their experts when assessing the subsequent disaster.

The other point of note was that, when she sailed for Le Havre, as there were no passengers there were only 75 stewards aboard. This meant that when the fire broke out, there were fewer crewmen available to fight the fire than there would have been on a normal voyage.

Shipboard gossip also mentioned earlier minor fires, but these were generally discounted, since most ships at that time suffered frequent minor outbreaks, generally due either to the system of wiring then in use, or to careless discarding of lit cigarettes.

Baker, a staunch anti-communist, was able to establish to his own satisfaction that the French Communist Party, at that time often accused of sabotage both within and outside France, were not involved in either of the fires on *Georges Philippar* or *L'Atlantique*.

The next day the *Daily Herald* featured a special piece from its Paris correspondent: "An amazing story told by M. de Bouraine [sic], a Cherbourg port official, has upset all the experts' opinions that *L'Atlantique* blaze was due to accident and not incendiarism.

"He has just revealed that he received an anonymous letter, posted *before* the fire broke out, announcing that the vessel would burst into flames. A similar anonymous letter is stated to have been received by the owners of the liner somewhat earlier. Bordeaux police are now on the track of a mysterious stranger, carrying a bulky despatch case, who was taken by taxi from Bordeaux to the port, where he boarded *L'Atlantique*. He returned to Bordeaux shortly afterwards with his despatch case empty, and has completely disappeared since."

Just after midnight on 7 January *L'Atlantique* was moored at the eastern end of the dock. The harbour fire brigade boarded and thoroughly doused the remaining fires. The fire crews found the bodies of the men asphyxiated near the boilers: later on they found the burnt remains of eight other crewmen. The company held a rollcall, and stated that of the 229 crew known to have boarded at Pauillac, 211 had been saved, with 18 lost.

The wreck was moved along the quay and moored near the maritime station. The lifeboat whose launch rope had burnt through still hung from the davits. The local fire brigade continued to pump water aboard to cool down the interiors, and cut the foremast level with the deck.

Still the Minister of the Merchant Marine refused to release the report into the *Georges Philippar* disaster, or to release preliminary findings on *L'Atlantique*. Newspaper editors in France and England started to publish articles asking why.

On 11 January lifeboat No.20 was found drifting off Barfleur and brought into Cherbourg: this was the boat first reported on 8 January. It had been stripped of most of its fittings and emergency provisions. A motorboat was found much later, on 5 May, in the North Sea.

The Times *correspondent in Paris filed a report on 11 January:*

L'Atlantique: Tribute to British rescuers

M. Léon Meyer, the Minister of Merchant Marine, appeared today before the relevant Committees of the Chamber and Senate with regard to the disaster to *L'Atlantique*. Official accounts of the proceedings state that both Committees decided to follow with the closest attention the course of the official enquiry.

The judicial enquiry into the disaster began there today. The most striking discovery so far made is that although the fire-proof doors were closed immediately after the discovery of the outbreak, another cabin which should have been protected by this action burst into flames soon afterwards. The discovery is one which goes to confirm the view generally held here that the rapid spread of the fire as well as its origin was due to some electrical defect.

Electrical Experiments

In an attempt to find a possible explanation of the disaster some electrical experts have just concluded some experiments here. They arranged a series of circuits wired in the manner prescribed by the regulations, that is to say, with the wires individually insulated, sheathed in metal and further insulated by battens of wood at suitable distances. Using an earth return they found that by producing a short circuit it was possible to heat the metal sheaths – not the wires themselves – to the point where the battens burst into flames, and not merely at one point but at many.

The tragic aspect of the disaster is to some extent redeemed by the report of Captain Schoofs on the splendid work done by the ships which came to the rescue of the survivors. He particularly praises the behaviour of the *Ford Castle* whose seamen, he reports, "added to their great professional skill a heroism worthy of the highest reward possible in such circumstances." He states that it was a boat from the British ship which, while the others held off at 500 yards from the burning wreck, approached to within 100 yards and picked up men without lifebelts who would otherwise have perished. This example induced others to approach, and in this way almost all the men who had been able to leave the ship were saved. The conduct of the seamen of the Dutch ship *Achilles* at this stage is also singled out for praise, one of their boats getting to within a few yards of the wreck in order to pick up a drowning man.

It was soon found that although the initial fires had started in Cabins 232 and 234, with the firefighters closely involved, another fire had started in Cabin 115 and went unnoticed. The investigators had seized the clocks from Cabins 232 and 115; the first had stopped at 3.55 and the second at 5.40, yet the fire alarm had been raised at 4.10. Another – unsubstantiated – report claimed the cabins had contained bedframes and bedsprings and not mattresses – metal parts that were not combustible.

There was an interesting letter from J.J. Eberll in the same Lloyd's List:
Sir,—I append a translation of the paragraph in the French hull policy covering abandonment to underwriters. The matter is of interest on the assumption that L'Atlantique *policy terms are in substance those of the standard French policy.*

Whenever the total amount of the cost of repairs exceeds 75% of the agreed value, and if in consequence the condemnation of the vessel is declared, the vessel must be regarded as unnavigable and may be abandoned to the Underwriters. (Credit must be given for the value of old sheathing or other wreckage, as well as for the difference between "new" and "old")

The only items that may be brought into account for the calculation of the 75% are the repairs resulting from perils of the sea, prescribed by the experts for putting the vessel again into good condition of navigability. Notably there may not be included any item for unforeseen expenses, wages and provisions of the crew, bottomry premium, expenses of surveys, or procedure or salvage, &c., nor temporary repairs.

From The Times, *Friday 13 January, from their Paris correspondent:*

Fire Danger in ships: New French rules

After consultation with experts and the directors of the leading shipping companies, M. Léon Meyer, the Minister of Merchant Marine, has decided to issue new and far more stringent regulations to be observed for the protection of ships against fire.

Administrative

1. Inspectors of shipping, when visiting vessels designed to carry more than 50 passengers, should be accompanied by an officer of the fire brigade, whose special task it will be to see that the defences of the ship against fire correspond as closely as possible to the demands of the London Convention of May 31, 1929.
2. Ships accommodating more than 250 passengers shall tell off from the crew a fire-fighting squad composed of three or six men, according to the size of the vessel, who have qualified for such duties after a period of training with professional firemen.
3. Ships of more than 15,000 tons gross shall carry three professional firemen. All fire-fighting squads are to be under the charge of a "security officer", who will see to the observance of the provisions of the London Convention.
4. In addition to the constitution of these special fire-fighting squads, particular attention will be paid to the instruction of candidates for entrance to the Merchant Marine in matters relating to security at sea.

Technical

1. The use of wood in the construction of ships is to be totally forbidden for stairways, lift shafts and cages, service ladders and for the bridge and wireless cabin, both of which must be entirely of metal. Where wooden panelling is used for gangways and passageways it shall be protected by asbestos. The ceilings of living quarters shall be made of non-inflammable material, and stanchions and deck beams if not of metal shall be insulated with asbestos or rendered fireproof in some other fashion. Decks must not be plank-lined in the interior of the ship; the use of parquet mey be later authorized, if it is isolated from the deck by asbestos sheeting.
2. Hangings and carpets are to be rendered as fireproof as possible by treatment. The use of rubber for floor covering will only be allowed if the material contains at least 75% of non-inflammable material.
3. Paints and varnishes: The use of such materials with nitro-cellulose basis is already forbidden. Details of permissible compounds and the fixing of a maximum permissible burning point will be given later.
4. The ventilation system shall be capable of immediate control from a central point.
5. The bridge and wireless cabin, in addition to being made entirely of metal, are to be designed in such a way as to resist fire to the utmost possible extent and should be capable of efficient ventilation in case of smoke. Ships of more than 10,000 tons shall carry two wireless cabins, each in a different part of the ship.

The regulations concluded with precise directions as to the wiring of electrical installations. The sheathing of all cables and wires is to be visible. Metal-covered cables and wires are to be fixed by means of metal collars and metal protectors attached to the hull, or where this is difficult they must be encased in wood, but covered with a metal sheath attached to the hull. Running repairs were to be carefully examined on arrival in port. Electrical fire-detection apparatus is to be carefully tested at frequent intervals.

Such of the foregoing regulations as are capable of being put into effect in ships now in commission will become effective immediately, or as soon as possible. All of them will apply to vessels now building or undergoing repairs.

Lloyd's List Wednesday 11 January: From Cherbourg, filed by The Daily Telegraph 9 January: Good progress has been made today with the work of restoring the steamer *L'Atlantique* to an even keel. The fire in the hold has been extinguished. There is reason to hope that it may be possible to transfer the vessel to dry dock tomorrow. Three more bodies, burned beyond recognition, have been found, making a total of eight. A representative of Lloyd's and the officials of the company owning the liner are meeting tomorrow to consider whether she can be reconstructed.

The Salvage Association's surveyor later reported: Have made preliminary examination. All passenger accommodation and structure A to F decks burnt out and ship side structure buckled to present water line. Engine and boiler rooms reported intact. Vessel now lying at new deep water quay.

Lloyd's List Thursday 12 Jan uary: From Cherbourg, filed January 10 by The Salvage Association's surveyor: Hope complete general survey of vessel tomorrow afternoon. Damage very serious, practically all structure above and including lower deck G destroyed, some damage also to engine and boiler rooms but not very serious.

St Catherine's Point reported a message from Niton Radio: Received from British motor vessel Upwey Grange: At 8.40am GMT, in lat. 50.9N, long. 1.24W, passed a waterlogged boat, danger to navigation; and at 9.50am GMT, in lat. 50.12N, long. 1.13W, passed another waterlogged boat, danger to navigation.

An interesting statement was made in *Shipbuilding & Shipping Record* for 12 January 1933: "The general design of large liners lends to the rapid spread of fire. The wide staircases and lift shafts act as funnels for its spread from deck to deck, while the long corridors induce rapid travel in the fore and aft direction."

On Thursday 12 January M. Meyer addressed a lengthy meeting of the Mercantile Marine Committee of the French Chamber of Deputies. After a long discussion, the Committee unanimously adopted a resolution recording its decision to make a careful and thorough examination of the matter.

M. Auguste Brunet was subsequently appointed to examine all reports, contracts and inquiries, from the laying down of the *Georges*

Philippar and *L'Atlantique* to the reports relating to the two fires, the first object being to fix responsibility, and the second being to ensure that liners in service, under construction or to be built shall embody the maximum guarantees for the safety of passengers and crews. The resolution added that after M. Brunet's report the Committee reserved the right to ask the Chamber for powers to inquire into the causes of the disaster.

M. Meyer [then] attended the meeting of the Marine Committee of the Senate and explained the position regarding the inquiries. According to the [French] newspaper *Le Temps*, the proposed measures were adopted at a meeting held at the Ministry of Merchant Marine on 9 January at which representatives of the leading ship-owning companies and shipyards, as well as Government officials, were present. This also called for the debate on the new Safety at Sea Bill, passed by the Chamber of Deputies on 19 June, 1931, to be placed on the agenda of the Senate as soon as possible.

As well as the previously-noted comments on the use of wood, paint, etc., they also called for any emergency repairs carried out to the various electrical circuits during a voyage to be carefully overhauled in port, and that electrical long-distance signalling and fire-detection equipment be constantly maintained in perfect condition and periodically tested under the direction of the Security Officer.

A small report in *The Times*, Friday 13 January, noted that "several small objects of unusual shape found in the cabins where the fire which destroyed the liner *L'Atlantique* originated have been identified as part of the electrical installation. The police have confiscated the electric clocks of these cabins".

A Paris report on 12 January was carried in Lloyd's List, 14 January:
French Minister condemns use of wood
As far as possible these new regulations will be made to apply not only to ships under construction but also to those in use at present. As a further precaution, fire brigades will be attached to all large liners.

By 14 January the administrative commission, headed by M. le Bourayne, had finished its investigation and returned to Paris.

Now a separate investigation was put in hand: M. Dumanois of the National Office for Combustible Liquids arrived to look into the handling and use of fuel oil on board the liner. Other experts brought in by the Chamber of Commerce began investigations on 16 January.

On 19 January the committee of experts published their report. Baker White in his book *Sabotage* succinctly summarised the findings: Upper part above C Deck, bulkheads, electrical installation, companion ways and furniture destroyed; boilers and turbines in good condition. Estimated cost of repairs 196,378,000 francs (£2.3m), rebuilding costs 208,000,000 francs (£2.45m). In the event of repairs and reconstruction being rejected, they advised it would be too costly to break her up, and that it would be better to sink her in deep water.

The same day Léon Meyer, in the French Senate on the Safety at Sea Bill, regarding the *L'Atlantique* tragedy, affirmed he still had "an open mind regarding the cause of the fire," and declared his determination "to do everything in future to ensure the safety of ships and those on board". To achieve this he outlined several measures, and then continbued: "The judicial inquiry is proceeding. I exclude no hypothesis, not even that of foul play. I have received some information on that subject. People are too ready to blame short circuits."

Schoofs was again interviewed in Paris on 15 February, during which he revealed that there had been several earlier attempts at sabotage. On one occasion a door that was only six feet above the water line had been unbolted and emery powder sprinkled into the machinery. If it had not been caught when it was, this could have needed repairs, delaying the sailing of the liner. However, he still felt that even if the fire aboard *L'Atlantique* had been set deliberately, he did not believe that the arsonist intended the destruction of the ship.

It was felt that the chief reception clerk on board *L'Atlantique*, M. Seignot, would be an important witness when he came before the examining magistrate at Bordeaux. It appeared he had visited Cabin 232 only 12 hours before the fire broke out, and didn't notice anything.

Replacement of L'Atlantique

Representations have been made to M. Léon Meyer by Bordeaux interests regarding the need for re-establishing communications between Bordeaux and Latin America, expresseing the wish that the replacement for *L'Atlantique* should be able to reach Bordeaux itself, and should have a speed which would place her in a favourable position as regards foreign competition. The Minister replied that his plans, which he would endeavour to bring to fruition as soon as possible, would comply with these suggestions.

L'Atlantique Inquiry: Previous fires disclosed

The Times *correspondent, Paris, 15 January:*
The members of the administrative committee which is inquiring into the fire in *L'Atlantique* returned to Bordeaux yesterday, after visiting the liner. In their inquiries they found no evidence that the fire was due to sabotage, but its possibility was not officially denied.

Three small fires occurred on board the ship before her last voyage. One was in the dynamo room, another in the bakery, the last being caused by a cigarette-end, which had been thrown on a carpet. These incidents are not considered to have had any special significance. The police, who are making separate investigations at Cherbourg, have found no trace of deliberate incendiarism in the cabins where the fire began, and rumours of mysterious behaviour on the part of various individuals are at present discounted. An expert committee of three members will meet at Cherbourg tomorrow to decide whether the ship can be repaired.

On 16 January, Lloyd's List carried further small reports:
A correspondent reported on 13 January: Reports received in Paris this evening from Bordeaux declare that it is now stated there that fire broke out on board *L'Atlantique* three times before she sailed for Havre. One outbreak, it is said, occurred in a cabin used as a darkroom for photographic work; another in offices on the second deck and a third in a storeroom filled with mattresses. The owners of the liner have so far made no comment on these allegations.

A Reuters report from Cherbourg dated 15 January:
Asked their opinion on the reports from Bordeaux that three previous fires had broken out in *L'Atlantique*, the police conducting the legal inquiry here frankly admitted that this was so, but added that they attached no significance to them. All three outbreaks were quickly mastered. One affected the engine-room, one the bakery, and the third a corridor where a lighted cigarette had been thrown on the carpet. They were, the police declared, "ordinary incidents" and happen time and again on board every liner.

On 20 January Lloyd's List carried a Reuter report: A motor launch from the steamer *L'Atlantique* picked up 15 miles out of Cherbourg, was handed over to the authorities here today by the Dutch steamer *Zaanam* (*? Stad Zaandam*), which arrived from Rotterdam. The launch, which was equipped with wireless, was capable of holding 28 persons.

Two reports from Cherbourg were carried in 20 January Lloyd's List:

The first stated that "None of the evidence which has been brought forward during the inquiry into the disaster provides any confirmation of the theory that the fire was the outcome of incendiarism. It is considered possible that a short circuit may have occurred in the cabin . . . the movement of the vessel, due to the rough weather . . may have caused the piles of mattresses to collapse . . . damaging the electric wires."

The second report concluded: ". . . it is possible that the wreck may be handed over to the Navy for carrying out technical experiments, after which it would be sunk."

The next day, 20 January, the *Morning Post* published an editorial leader drawing attention to the failure to publish the report on the loss of the *Georges Philippar*. That afternoon the Paris correspondent for the paper, George Martelli, attended the Chamber of Deputies and read the article to the Assembly. M. Léon Meyer assured everyone that he would give serious consideration to taking whatever steps appeared to be necessary. He also stated that he would pass a copy of the final report to the British Government.

M. Meyer was questioned in the National Assembly by seven deputies, MM. Philibert Besson, Antoine Cayrel, Philippe Henriot, Luden Midol, Auguste Raynaud, René Richard and Henri Tasso. They were charged with establishing the causes of the tragedy, and to develop safety measures for the future.

During the discussions, M. Richard cited from a letter published in the newspaper *L'Intransigeant*, in which a passenger who had made two earlier crossings on *L'Atlantique* had written in expressing his concern at the inherent dangers of a serious fire aboard the liner.

He then referred to a letter published on Friday 6 January in a morning newspaper, *L'Action Française*, which referred to a letter written some months previously by Jacques Aguttes, who had been a second lieutenant on *L'Atlantique*, to Chargeur Réunis. Aguttes had resigned after a career of thirty years, saying he no longer felt that he could guarantee the safety of his passengers, and that the modern liner was regarded more as an hotel than as a ship.

It was claimed in the letter that the Captain and the officer of the watch did not have keys to certain parts of the ship, that there were areas accessible only to the 'hotel director'. This meant that when the fire watch patrolled certain areas, they were unable to ensure that those areas behind the locked doors were actually safe.

Deputy René Richard then read out a letter from Georges Philippar, president of the Cie. Messageries Maritimes (after whom the ill-fated vessel was named), which emphasised the dangers of wood used in the panelling of the gangways. M. Philippar also referred to the amount of soft wood used as battens on which the panelling was mounted, the wood panelling on the stairways, and the wood cladding used in the ceilings of the various passageways.

A report from Commander Watremez of the Paris fire brigade submitted a report which was read into the minutes. He referred to the effect of the gaps between the ceiling cladding and the deck above, and the similar gaps behind the wall panels. These were used to conceal

the multitude of wires, cables, pipes and conduits, but in the event of a fire, they would also act as funnels along which flames and hot air and smoke could travel very quickly in all directions.

There were no fire stops or metal blocks anywhere within this labyrinth of tunnels. When the fire broke out, even as the firefighters were busy fighting the visible flames in the cabins, other flames were passing over and around them behind the panelling, completely unseen.

Deputy René Richard summarised steps he felt were necessary to take to prevent another tragedy on board a French liner. These included the use of partitions in the ceilings, non-flammable materials with a matching reduction in the use of wood, use of paints and varnishes with lower flammability, additional radio rooms in alternative areas of the ship, specially trained firefighters within the crew with relief crews available, the adoption of 110V alternating current on board using electric cabling within metal conduits, and the installation of more sensitive smoke detectors.

He concluded by saying that recently the emphasis for new liners had been on increasing luxury and speed, and that this should now be replaced by concentrating on safety.

Another Deputy, M. Besson, then took the floor of the National Assembly. He claimed that fires were common on most ships, and then made a claim that there had been six previous fires on *L'Atlantique*. However, no substantive proof or evidence was given for this claim, and investigations with members of the crew and dockyard workers could not support the allegation.

M. Besson noted the firefighting equipment already aboard large liners of the day, and expressed amazement that with all the modern technology available, such fires could still occur. His conclusion was that the recent fires were the result of sabotage or some evil force intent on destroying the French merchant marine.

He alluded to three different fires on *Paris*, insisting this supported his contention of foul play, and referred to the fire on *Georges Philippar*, asserting that there were two centres to the fire. He then commented on the outbreaks on *L'Atlantique* on different decks, especially on the fire seen forward by Gaston as he was escaping up a ladder.

He insisted the one common aspect to the spate of recent fires on French vessels was the electrical wiring, and in particular the danger from overloading and short circuits. He alleged that if fuses were replaced by higher-rated components, it would be comparatively easy for the wiring to overheat and the trunking to catch fire. Simple measures could reduce this risk, such as running the wiring in metal conduits and putting fuses in locked boxes so they cannot be tampered with by unauthorised peolpe.

The conclusion of the Assembly was that whilst no single factor seemed sufficient to have destroyed *L'Atlantique*, the combination had been too much to control. The excessive use of wood, the use of nitro-cellulose paints and varnishes, untreated carpets, too few crew to act as firefighters, the broad central street of shops and the lack of sufficient fire detection equipment all contributed.

The experts called in by the Commercial Tribunal next reported: in their opinion the hull, inner structures and engines had not been

severely damaged, and they considered that the cost of repair and reconstruction would be between 196m francs and 208m francs.

Sud Atlantique carefully considered the Tribunal's report, and finally on 6 February asked the Tribunal to pass a ruling that *L'Atlantique* was no longer economic to repair, and that the company could pass the wreck to the insurers; this was granted. "At the request of Captain Schoofs the vessel was today condemned by the Tribunal as no longer fit for navigation. The company's legal adviser will now inform the insurance companies of this decision and notify them that the company will hand over the wreck to the Underwriters." The insured value of the liner was given as £1,150,000 for ordinary risk, and an additional £850,000 in the event of a total loss. The insurers were unhappy at this prospect, and requested Harland & Wolff in Belfast to prepare a bid for the rebuilding costs, to compare with Sud Atlantique's figures.

On 9 February Lloyd's List carried a Reuter report: The remarkable statement that the crew of the *L'Atlantique* did not know how to deal with fire at sea has been made by Colonel Pouderoux, head of the Paris Fire Brigade and one of the members of the administrative Committee of Inquiry. "As for the seamen," he said to the *Paris-Midi*, "they were undoubtedly courageous but lacked experience. It was evident that they did not know how to extinguish a fire completely."

According to a Reuter report, on 11 February, Schoofs was again questioned at Bordeaux by the examining magistrate considering the

---

An amusing small piece was printed in Lloyd's List on 20 January:

French awards to British Seamen

Surprise awaited the mate and four members of the crew of the *Ford Castle* when that vessel arrived at Sunderland yesterday from Havre. There the mate had received a gold watch and the others silver watches for their gallantry in taking men from the burning French liner *L'Atlantique*. The Sunderland Customs official demanded duty on these articles, but the men demurred – and the watches were put under seal pending negotiations with the Chief Customs officials in London. The Press Association was later informed by the Customs Authorities that the delivery of the watches to the men had been allowed, and that they would therefore be returned without payment of duty.

Once the fire had been completely extinguished, the Cherbourg Fire Brigade sent in an expert team to investigate the likely sources. These two photographs, from Richard Faber's collection, show the damage inside the cabins where the firemen determined that the fire started.

*The photographs taken by the Cherbourg 'pompiers' show the utter
devastation they found on board. They concentrated on the likelihood of
the ship's movement in the heavy swell causing chafing of the electrical
wires where they passed through the bulkheads.*

report of the Committee of Inquiry. Asked afterwards if he still believed that the fire had been caused by foul play, the captain answered: "It is only a hypothesis, nevertheless what is disturbing is that the fire broke out at four different places and this fact certainly points to criminal handiwork.

In February, Martelli re-interviewed Schoofs who still held firmly to the sabotage theory. This he based on the fact that the fire broke out in adjoining cabins, that a short-circuit was unlikely since the lights were off, and that the cabins only stored mattresses. Soon after, the inquiry by the Bordeaux police also agreed with the sabotage theory.

The longer the hulk stayed alongside the pier, the more derelict and desolate she became.
No-one was prepared to accept the responsibility for even the most basic maintenance.

On 13 February Maître Dor, legal counsel for Sud Atlantique, issued a formal statement. "Sud Atlantique has today given notice to the 72 companies who are insurers of *L'Atlantique* of the abandonment of the ship to them by the shipowners, who, taking their stand on the valuation of the surveyors and the judgment of the Cherbourg Tribunal of Commerce, relinquish the wreck to the insurers, and require them to pay the sum assured, 170 million francs."

Then in mid-February, M. de Bourayne went on public record, stating:

"As a result of minute examination of the evidence, I have become convinced that the fire was not due to a short circuit nor to carelessness. It was probably caused by petrol sprinkled on the carpets of several adjoining cabins and deliberately set on fire.

Up to date no suspicion has been directed against any particular person and a large number of witnesses, for the most part members of the crew, have still to be examined. I put forward the suggestion that the authors of the fire may be acting for some national or international organisation."

In February the local magistrate, M. Carle, announced that he would be closely questioning the four men who were nearest to the source of the fire – the sweeper Ferrugia, the telephonist Raimandia, plus the night watchman and the senior night watchman.

After the panel of three experts had ruled on the state of the wreck, the insurers called for a second examination, in particular of the underwater section of the hull. If it could be proved that the hull was sound, any repair costs would be substantially reduced, since the repair work would be internal rather than structural.

Later M. de Bourayne said it appeared that the fire had started in two groups of cabins, numbers 228 and 230, and in 232 and 234. These two groups were separated by a metal fire-proof partitioning which curiously had suffered only minor fire damage.

The doors of the cabins in which the fire started were locked. An effort was made to open them, but the pass key of the night watchman broke in the lock of the first cabin and they could not be opened until the chief watchman was found with another key.

Members of the crew were emphatic that at first there was no water pressure in the fire hoses. They were equally emphatic that the fires were in the cabins themselves and not inside the cabin walls.

There had been fifty electrically-controlled alarm signals installed in *L'Atlantique*, but no members of the crew had admitted to hearing any of them. Warning of the fire was passed by word of mouth, even to the Captain on the bridge. The member of the crew, a sweeper from Corsica named Ferrugia, who discovered the fire, was said to have gone up to the bridge himself.

On 14 February Lloyd's List carried a Reuter's report: In regard to the salvage question, Maître Dor says that the reports of the various salvors filed with the Cherbourg Commercial Court showed that they all worked to the best of their ability in very trying and dangerous circumstances, and did not fight among themselves for possession of the wreck. They were now very rightly following a policy of wait and see. The amount of salvage remuneration will largely depend upon the value of what is left of *L'Atlantique* and therefore the question as to whether *L'Atlantique* should be repaired or merely sold for breaking up was of immense interest for the salvors.

During M. Seignot's evidence to the examining magistrate at the official inquiry at Bordeaux, he confirmed he visited cabin 232 on the afternoon before the fire erupted, but he found nothing abnormal.

He stated: "Although fire also broke out in cabin 115, some distance from the original seat of the outbreak, this was an hour and a half after the first alarm had been given, and might well have simply been an extension of the first blaze."

The Ministry of Public Works authorised the harbourmaster at Cherbourg to order the removal of the wreck within the following two weeks. This instruction was made to Sud Atlantique, who declined any responsibility, since they had abandoned the wreck to the insurers. The insurers, in turn, declined the order, since they had refused to accept the abandonment of the wreck.

Lack of progress in reaching a settlement forced Maître Dor to issue a public statement on 24 February that unless the insurers paid out in full before 13 March, he would apply to the Paris Commercial Court for a writ against the underwriters.

On 3 March 1933 it was announced that Sud Atlantique was to hand over the wreck to the insurers, and that they were claiming the 170m francs (around £2m at that time) insurance payout. This had been broken down into the following approximate figures due from each insurance market: Paris 69m francs, Bordeaux 5m francs, New York 20m francs, Hamburg 0·2m francs and Great Britain 76m francs. Many of the Paris underwriters had subscribed on behalf of English companies, and most of the French underwriters had re-insured on the London market. This meant the bulk of any payout would be carried by the markets in London and Liverpool.

A stand-off developed. Sud Atlantique had the right to hand over the wreck in this way, but equally the insurers had the right to refuse to accept it until they were satisfied with the outcome of all the investigations. If these showed a fault in the construction or the wiring for example, then the cost would be levied elsewhere. They had one month to decide whether to pay up or challenge the abandonment.

On 18 March George Martelli again interviewed Schoofs, who insisted he gave the wireless operator, Creach, two separate orders to send out messages. The first, at about 4.30am, when he was still hoping to control the fire, gave the ship's position and a statement that the ship was on fire. About an hour later, on his way back to the bridge to organise 'Abandon Ship', he insisted he shouted to the operator to send an SOS message.

Schoofs was adamant that Creach was able to send out several messages before the radio room filled with smoke, and that the SOS messages were heard at Le Havre. Schoofs totally rebutted Creach's account that he was not aware of a fire or any problems before 5.45am, as the operator had claimed to the previous enquiry. Schoofs still held to his sabotage theory.

The foremast distorted and collapsed due to the intense heat from the fire, but was not removed until some time after the hulk was docked.

Enquiries were made of the various wireless stations along the Channel. All agreed – no messages had been received. Breville (?) categorically denied Schoofs' claim of a 'feeble signal' being picked up. The earliest message on record was that received by Niton on the Isle of Wight, transmitted by the *Ruhr*.

On 12 March more bones were found on board. Some were near the butcher's, but were later found to be animal bones from carcasses on board. The others were found to be human bones, in the cabin of the second officer. A fresh inquiry was initiated by officials from Bordeaux. They hired M. Bourdon to look into the possibility of the fire having started in several places through sabotage, rather than in the one cabin.

On 19 March Sud Atlantique formally filed an action in the Paris Courts against the insurance companies, claiming the full 170 million francs. At that time the British underwriters had still not received formal notice of the abandonment of the wreck, although action was put in hand to correct that.

The authorities at Cherbourg were concerned at the extended stay of the hulk. It was still moored at the quay, and was not a welcoming sight for international arrivals. It was occupying a prime site, which the harbour authorities needed. It was becoming urgent to decide where to keep the wreck until the arguments were resolved.

Special Commissioner Liger from Boulogne was charged on 26 March 1933 with conducting an inquest into the cause or causes of the fire aboard *L'Atlantique*. As part of his investigations, he enlisted the help of London's Scotland Yard, requesting them to investigate a named person and to look into any possible involvement.

The allegation was made that in December 1932 this person attempted to hire an unemployed Englishman to get a package on board a liner in France. In spite of much pressure, the Englishman refused, even though he was offered false documentation and a lot of money to pursue the matter. The inquiry team were convinced as to the authenticity of these claims, and used this to assert that an 'international organisation' was intent on destroying the French merchant marine.

> *A subsequent Reuter report noted:*
> Four extraordinary facts which throw a sinister light on *L'Atlantique* disaster are reported by the Bordeaux correspondent of *Le Matin*.
>
> 1 The day before *L'Atlantique* sailed on what was to be her last voyage, M. de Bourayne, now president of the Administrative Commission of Inquiry, received a letter, it is revealed, saying that fire would break out in the liner between Pauillac and Havre.
>
> 2 There have, it appears, been three recent outbreaks of fire in *L'Atlantique*.
>
> 3 An act of sabotage directed against the steering apparatus took place.
>
> 4 Three days before the vessel sailed, an unknown man hailed a taxi at Bordeaux, driven by a chauffeur who is a retired detective. The chauffeur put him down by *L'Atlantique* in the Pauillac Docks. He went on board with a bulky dispatch case and returned 25 minutes later with the same dispatch case empty. No-one knows who it was in *L'Atlantique* who received the mysterious visitor.

It has to be remembered that as soon as *L'Atlantique* had arrived at Cherbourg, three independent commissions had been set up to investigate the disaster.

The first commission, by the maritime authorities at Cherbourg, was charged to submit an official report to the Ministry of Merchant Marine. The second commission was to look into the technical aspects of the outbreak of the fire and how it spread so quickly. The third commission was to consolidate all the information gathered from the various sources and to produce a comprehensive report into the tragedy.

The President of the Administrative Inquest Commission, M. de Bourayne, submitted his report to the Minister of the Merchant Marine on 30 March 1933, in favour of sabotage, ruling out any question of short circuits. Following this, the presiding judge at Bordeaux, M. de Courlanges, charged a local examining judge, M. Carle, with gathering evidence with a view to charging an unnamed person with sabotage.

With still no agreement reached, Maître Dor called on the Tribunal of Commerce in Paris on Monday, 27 March to fix an early date for a settlement to be reached. The Courts fixed the following Monday for a decision, with judgement to follow soon after. The court papers still only cited the French underwriters, although the original insurance contract included a clause that the English underwriters would follow any lead given by their French counter-parts.

Maître Dor called for an order for pro rata payments to be made initially. The insurers countered with the claim that the Commercial Tribunal was not competent to resolve many of the matters, and that as they were not represented when the experts estimated the cost of repairs initially, the Court should appoint a new set of experts to resolve the costs, and that there should be an open invitation for ship repairers to tender for the work.

Initial statements were made on 3 April, with Léopold Dor representing Sud Atlantique and Attorney Prodomides representing the insurers. By now the various British insurers had agreed to be represented through the presence at the hearing of the leading London underwriter that was named on the policy. Maître Dor accepted that the initial estimate of 196m francs for the repair of the liner was not a final figure, but he challenged whether or not tenders could be asked for from repairers in other countries, arguing that *L'Atlantique* was a French liner, and an ambassador of French taste and design. If the repair work were given to another country, the rebuild would reflect that country's tastes and workmanship, which would not reflect well on France.

The shell of the Grand Salon: in the foreground can be seen the remains of one of the occasional tables. See the picture on page 33, which shows this table in its original glory. Behind the table is the statue of Samothrace.

He also pointed out that if the insurers paid the full amount to Sud Atlantique, they would use the money to have a new ship built in a French yard, providing employment and reflecting yet again all that was best in France.

In April the Court ruled that they were competent to hear the case for total loss as well as that for insurance on the hull and machinery, since both were linked by the abandonment clauses. However the Court also ruled that the facts of the fire were still not fully clarified, and that they felt it was necessary to order another survey before reaching a verdict.

The experts appointed were Briquart, Pugnet and Ravier, who were charged by the court with examining the liner and declaring whether or not she could be repaired, and if so at what cost, and to report their findings back to the Court. No ruling was made on the question of obtaining tenders for any repairs although it was implicit.

On 29 April Lloyd's List reported: "Following repeated protests from the Cherbourg Chamber of Commerce, the hulk of *L'Atlantique*, which had been lying since January off the Quai de France, opposite the new maritime railway station, has been towed to the northern section of the dock, where it will not be a hindrance to traffic."

On Sunday 7 May 1933 Schoofs and Gaston were decorated by Governor General Olivier with the highest decorations of the Central Society for Ocean Salvage. Held during the General Assembly of the Society in the amphitheatre of the Sorbonne in Paris, 5,000 people watched and applauded as the awards were announced. Captain Schoofs was awarded the vermilion medal of the Society: the accompanying speech paid tribute to the example Captain Schoofs gave to others, and the many initiatives he took to save lives and attempt to salvage the liner.

Captain Gaston also received the vermilion medal: testament was given to the Assembly detailing the many attempts he made to rescue people on board, in spite of suffering from smoke inhalation, and then his example to others in jumping overboard and swimming to the rescue boats.

The vermilion medal was also awarded to Lieut Even: the speech acknowledged not only his bravery in helping to fight the fire, but also that he returned as one of the volunteers, and his attempt to re-board *L'Atlantique*, during which his leg had been crushed.

A vermilion medal was awarded posthumously to Hector Courrie, who also was awarded the François Provensal prize. His efforts in fighting the fire, saving several sailors and his final effort to close a fire door, which was to cost him his life, were detailed to a silent assembly. He was also awarded the citation of the Order of the Nation for his bravery.

The bodies found on board the wreck were carefully placed in coffins and taken ashore, to the new Maritime Station, an area of which had been set aside as a temporary chapel.

Tragically some of the bodies could not be identified, as they were too badly burnt. A brief service was held at the chapel by Abbé Guyard, from Saint Clement, before the coffins were taken to the Pasteur Hospital, where they remained until they left for Bordeaux on 12 January.

A service had been held at the hospital for families and friends, with representatives from the government, the city of Cherbourg, the shipping companies and the naval and merchant marine.

Those bodies that could be identified were returned to their families; for those that could not, it was decided to include them in a common grave. Sud Atlantique bought a plot from the Charterhouse Cemetery in Bordeaux, and finally on 14 November 1933 seven coffins were interred.

Two of these contained warehouseman René Madic and the carpenter Berjot, another two contained identified bodies, a fifth coffin contained three more unidentified bodies, and the sixth contained the ashes of a further three unidentified bodies.

The seventh coffin was that of Pierre Millet, the head boilerman, who had no family and was therefore buried with his shipmates. Among those known to have been aboard but lost in the fire were Andrea Bouquet, Pierre Millet, René Madic, Pierre Cajoles, Jean Cadilhou and François Labeyrie.

Captain Schoofs stands forlornly on the quayside beside the hulk.

Supporting sponsors keep the hulk upright whilst it was in the drydock, during the examination by the various experts.

The company asked the insurers for payment of 100,120,000 francs for the hull and the equipment, and a further 70,780,000 for the "total loss", a total of 170,900,000 francs. The insurers in return claimed that the second sum claimed had already been thrown out by an arbitration court, and that the main amount could only be claimed if it could be proved that that the insurers were both responsible for and liable to make such payment.

The basis of the insurers' defence was that they could only be required to pay for any repairs and rebuilding if this was less than the amount insured, and this was the limit of their liability. However, if the cost of rebuilding was more than the amount insured, then the owners had the right to surrender the wreck to the insurers and demand the full amount of 170,900,000 francs.

Of the 69 insurance companies involved in the total insurance coverage, most were based in the United Kingdom; these insisted that a dockyard in the United Kingdom could effect the repairs for less than the insured sum.

The three experts appointed by the Court reported on 8 May 1933, admitting that no new clues had been found regarding the cause of the fire, but stating that the hull had been badly distorted by the heat of the fire, and that repairs would cost at least 190m francs, and were therefore not viable. This conclusion was based on a report from M. Barthelemy, a military marine engineer, whose team had been appointed by the experts to assess the state of the hull.

The debris accumulating from the wreck was due to have been taken in sealed wagons to Bordeaux for further examination, but on 22 May it was decided that M. Berger would examine the material on site, only removing anything he found that he felt was of interest.

The maritime station at Cherbourg was part of a complete rebuild of the harbour and its infrastructure, started in 1923, aimed at rivalling the facilities at Le Havre. Two new jetties were constructed and overall the harbour area was greatly increased. By 1928 this work was completed, and they started on the Maritime Station and embarkation hall. Designed by René Levavasseur, the main hall was in the contemporary art deco style, while immediately behind it the railway terminus had 45 tracks, capable of handling a tremendous throughput of passengers and cargo.

Before the new station could be officially opened, however, the disaster of *L'Atlantique* occurred. The first great liner to be docked at the quay was the burnt-out hulk, and the first customers of the terminus were the charred bodies of the unfortunate sailors who died on board. With the inauguration ceremony approaching, it was becoming increasingly important to put *L'Atlantique* somewhere while the arguments were resolved, so that the harbour could get back to a semblance of normality. The Cherbourg Chamber of Commerce proposed that the wreck should be towed to the naval harbour, but the naval authorities objected to this on several grounds, suggesting instead that the wreck should lie in the roadstead.

Lloyd's List of 6 June carried a report by *The Times* correspondent: "The director of the Co. Sud Atlantique and the experts who were charged to examine the wreck of the steamer *L'Atlantique* have advised M. Pierre Appell, the Under-Secretary of State for Public Works, that it will be possible to tow the wreck to St. Nazaire. As an examination in dock is necessary, this operation will take place as soon as a dock is ready to receive it, probably towards 20 June."

The same issue also reported: "The experts charged with examining the wreck of the steamer *L'Atlantique* have decided that this can only be done at St. Nazaire, where she was built. The vessel therefore will be towed back to St. Nazaire about 20 June, when it is expected the weather will be favourable."

Lloyd's List of 10 June carried a further *Times* report: "Behind the announcement that the French liner *L'Atlantique* is to be towed from Cherbourg to St. Nazaire this month lies another important development. It is understood that the experts appointed by the

Commercial Tribunal have decided, after several discussions with the representatives of the insurance companies concerned, that ship repairers may be invited to inspect the vessel when she arrives at St. Nazaire with a view to submitting tenders for repairing the liner."

Approaches were made to the French navy to allow the hulk to be towed to the Homet dry dock in the main harbour, but the naval authorities declined. In early June it was proposed to tow *L'Atlantique* back to St Nazaire for a thorough examination. This would enable any ship repairers interested in tendering for the work the chance to thoroughly inspect the hull.

By 14 June plan for the tows were ready, with the lower portholes carefully cemented up, and they were waiting for favourable weather. *Lloyd's List* announced on 16 June: "Preparations are being made to tow *L'Atlantique* to St. Nazaire. The voyage will begin, weather permitting, about June 25, and will take about 5 days. A launch fitted with wireless apparatus will be placed on board in case of accident."

On 19 June M. Leygues, by then the Minister of Marine, agreed that the hulk could be moored in the large dock near the arsenal, as the British underwriters had objected to the tow to St. Nazaire. By 29 June several firms had put in initial tenders for the repair work, and on 30 June several engineers representing British shipyards interested in the work arrived at Cherbourg, to find that she was still not in a dry dock for them to examine the hull.

It was then proposed that in order to free up the main quay and to enable the President to open the new maritime station at the end of July, that the hulk should moored out in the roads, at the cost and risk of the owners. This idea was firmly rejected by the various companies involved in the salvage exercise, as they had still not received any payments for their efforts.

On 21 June *Reuter's* reported: "It has been decided to drydock the burned-out hulk of *L'Atlantique* at Cherbourg. She will be moved from the Quai de France to the big Le Homet Dry Dock where she can be more easily examined by the experts next week."

On 18 July it was announced that in consideration of an advance of 300,000 francs made to the French Navy, and a pledge to take all responsibility for the operation, Sud Atlantique obtained a promise that the hulk could be moved on 20 or 21 July to the Homet naval dry dock in Cherbourg. They agreed that it would be for no longer than a fortnight, after which she would have to be moored either out in the roads or perhaps towed to a nearby harbour.

In the morning of Thursday 20 July she was moved to the 800 foot long Homet dry dock by five tugs, for hull damage and deformations to be assessed. Moving the wreck was handled by Captain Pichard, using three of the Abeille tugs that had performed so well during the original salvage operation. The operation was completed by 8.00am, and the dock had drained by 4.00pm.

Initial examinations didn't show any major deformation, although M. Nizery, a director of Sud Atlantique, found what he described as 'a noticeable distortion of the keel' when he examined the bottom. During the liner's brief career, *L'Atlantique* was known to have touched bottom several times, which could have accounted for some of this.

Lloyd's List of 22 July carried a Reuter report from Cherbourg: "The expert who inspected the burnt-out hull of *L'Atlantique* which was towed into the Naval Dockyard here this morning, refuses to disclose the result of his examination. It is stated, however, that the lower part of the hull below the waterline is intact. No damage is apparent, and even the paint is not impaired."

The following day a statement was issued stating that the keel was found to be arched, with a difference of 16 inches between the midship portion and the ends, confirming initial calculations made by experts some months previously. It was thought this would be enough to support Sud Atlantique's claims that the distortion was sufficient to make repairs uneconomic.

Shortly after, on 30 July 1933, the French President, Albert Lebrun, officially opened the new facilities for the port of Cherbourg.

The time limit that had been agreed for the stay in the dry dock was then extended, to allow the experts appointed by the Commercial Court to examine the hull. The main expert, Mr Lister, was due to arrive on 3 August. On 28 August Sud Atlantique asked for a further extension as the Courts had still not delivered a verdict. The Minister of Marine refused to grant any extension, and the company was asked to remove the hulk immediately. However, as Sud Atlantique had formally abandoned her, and the insurers had refused to accept her, nobody knew who was responsible for the removal or further handling of the hulk.

A public announcement was made on 1 August of further awards to several of the *L'Atlantique*'s crew. Captain Schoofs was made an officer in the Legion d'Honneur. Second Captain Gaston and Lieutenants Even and Hué were made Knights of the Legion, and Hector Courrie was posthumously awarded the same honour.

A report in Lloyd's List on 5 August alleged that "it had been decided to take advantage of the extended stay in the dry dock to careen the vessel, and that the hull will then be examined more closely and repainted."

Lloyd's List carried a report in its issue of 29 August: "Experts appointed by the Seine Tribunal of Commerce are understood to have come to the conclusion that the French liner *L'Atlantique* is beyond repair. This reported finding is subsequent to that of the Cherbourg Commercial Tribunal, which, in the absence of the insurer's representatives, found that *L'Atlantique* was beyond repair and that the owners were entitled to abandon her."

On 4 September naval authorities pointed out that the hulk had stayed much longer than the agreed two weeks, and that it should be removed. However, no-one was prepared to accept the responsibility of deciding where it should go, or how to move it. In September experts agreed the extent of the hull deformation.

The navy, owed ever-increasing rent which no-one would pay, wanted her out: the harbour authorities, desperate to improve their international image, also wanted her out. By 22 October tenders from various British shipyards had been submitted.

On 15 November the Ministry of Marine gave formal notice to Sud Atlantique to remove the hulk from the dry dock, although a period of bad weather immediately made them suspend the instruction. The Commercial Tribunal had still not passed down its verdict, and Sud Atlantique had already had to pay 750,000 francs towards charges levied by the Ministry for the use of the dock.

The structural experts presented their official findings to the court on 24 November – a two to one majority said that the ship could not be economically repaired, and unanimously agreed that the cost of such repairs would exceed the limit of 100,000,000 francs, allowing Sud Atlantique to abandon the liner to the insurers under the terms of the insurance, as the cost equalled or exceeded the insured value. The insurers still insisted that the repairs were possible in England at a figure somewhat less than the limit.

The next court hearing was held on 10 December 1933, when Sud Atlantique again pressed for payment in full from the insurers, and the legal abandonment of the wreck. The insurance companies in turn presented to the court an estimate for repairs from Harland & Wolff in Belfast, who proposed that they could complete the repairs for 98m francs. On this basis the insurers asked the court to reject Sud

Atlantique's petition and to order a settlement of their original offer of 100,120,000 francs.

However, the court rejected the Harland and Wolff tender, as it did not include an agreement that the ship would be put back to the state it had been in before the fire.

A short article in *Shipbuilding and Shipping Record* of 11 January 1934 detailed briefly the various tenders received. These included Harland & Wolff's tender of £1,240,000 (97,960,000 francs), within the insured value. Cammell Laird tendered £1,343,000, while Workman Clark failed to tender, claiming the specifications were incomplete.

Ironically, at the time of tendering the exchange rate for the franc was 79 to the pound, but by the time it was under consideration the franc had fallen to 83 to the pound, which made it more than the insured value. The tender had a 14-day acceptance clause, so it was time-expired anyway.

On 29 March 1934 the UK *Daily Mail* published a further two articles on the whole disaster.

The first story concerned the appeal lodged by the insurers.

The *Daily Mail*, on inquiry in Paris and London, learns that the underwriters concerned are to press with the utmost vigour their appeal against the decision of the Paris Commercial Court ordering them to pay £2,000,000 odd in respect of the 'total loss' of the French liner *L'Atlantique* destroyed by fire in the English Channel on January 4, 1933.

It is understood that as the result of long investigation the underwriters' representatives have secured possession of documentary evidence which in their view proves conclusively that important facts were withheld from them when they were asked to renew the insurance of the vessel.

In support of this there is other documentary evidence from members of the staff of *L'Atlantique*, all of which will be submitted to the French Court of Appeal for its consideration.

The appeal was lodged yesterday and the action will be one of the most important maritime issues ever decided.

The second story can be attenuated as follows:

"... a few days ago detectives on the trail of some missing jewels stumbled on the mysterious movements of a party of Englishmen, both in Geneva and across the Jura Mountains in France.

Those Englishmen were Londoners. They were in Geneva last December in connection with the investigations into the mysterious destruction of the liner *L'Atlantique*. Their investigations were set on foot by the insurance companies concerned.

Part of the insurance companies' case is a number of documents proving conclusively faulty construction in the liner. These documents were in the possession of a Frenchman who had intimated his willingness to part with them – at a price.

That they were available was known not only to the representatives of the insurance companies – the mysterious Englishmen – but also to question which party would get in first and pay the higher figure, The Frenchman had decided on a little tenement in a back street of Champagnolle, in the Jura Mountains, as the place of negotiation.

The Englishmen reached Geneva only to find a blizzard raging and the roads across the frontier well nigh impassable. They got hold of a car driver who was willing to take the risk. At last they reached the Frenchman's door.

He demanded a sum far beyond that which the visitors were in a position to pay. They returned to Geneva for further consultations. The following day the negotiators once more set out for Champagnolle. Still the blizzard raged. When they at last reached the town it was to learn that two Frenchmen had arrived and were in the house.

They hurried to the Frenchman's house to find that it was his wife who was dealing with the other men. Without a moment's delay they came to terms with the man, and while, in the next room, their rivals bickered with the woman, they carried the precious documents off in triumph.

Those papers are now safely in London and will form an important part of the insurance companies' case when their appeal comes before the Paris courts in a few weeks' time."

In Lloyd's List of 18 January, it was reported that a French steamer, *Taillefer*, from Nantes, had picked up another of *L'Atlantique*'s boats off Cotentin.

The court declared its ruling on 22 January 1934, accepting in full the judgement of the various experts appointed, and requiring the insurers to pay out in full the figure of 170,900,000 francs plus all expenses and interest accrued since 15 March 1933.

One such cost which still hadn't been agreed was that of the rent for the quay at Homet from the Navy at 7,000 francs a day. By the date of the court ruling, this had risen to 1,250,000 francs, but no one knew to whom the bill should be sent.

The insurers tried another appeal in February, basing their claim on the fact that the verdict of the experts had not been unanimous. The Court of Appeal in Paris gave the matter long and careful scrutiny, but on 28 December 1934 they upheld the original decision.

Meanwhile on 4 October 1934 the French magazine *L'Intransigeant* published an interview with the magistrate overseeing the inquiry into the causes of the fire, M. d'Uhalt. One interesting piece quoted him as saying: "I shall examine an allegation of malicious sabotage during the installation of the electrical system". The article went on to claim that all the workmen employed on the original electrical installation were to be interviewed.

Soon after, confirmation came from Paris, with the statement: "The examining magistrate has been instructed to begin questioning some 200 workmen who had been employed by the various companies involved in the electrical installations".

Increasingly, people were comparing the fire on *L'Atlantique* with that on *Georges Philippar* – both had been built in the same yards using similar materials and basically the same workmen.

However, other experts pointed out that whilst *Georges Philippar* had been lost on her maiden voyage, *L'Atlantique* had completed several extensive crossings to South America, and that if anything had been sabotaged during the construction, it would have shown up earlier.

Then in November drama erupted at the Appeal Court in Paris, which was hearing the appeal by the insurers against the earlier decision in favour of Sud Atlantique. Maître Chresteil suddenly introduced new evidence: the French police, investigating a separate matter, had cause to interview a Frenchman who had been reported as acting strangely.

Inspector Charpentier discovered that the man was the French representative of the British manufacturer of the gyroscopic compass and automatic pilot fitted to *L'Atlantique*.

The lawyer read into the court minutes the police report of their interview: "Before *L'Atlantique*'s last voyage I went on board to test the apparatus. I found that it was in perfect order, but the electrical installation on which it depended was defective. I reported this to London to protect them should *L'Atlantique* experience any problem resulting from a failure of either the gyro compass or the automatic pilot."

On 23 November Maître Chresteil delivered another dramatic statement, claiming that the insulation of much of the cabling on *L'Atlantique* had a resistance of only 4,000 ohms, whereas the Bureau Veritas required 500,000 ohms. The lawyer claimed that the failure of Sud Atlantique to

Top: *The utter devastation on the foredeck.*

Lower: *The devastation on the promenade deck.*

disclose this risk to the insurers annulled the policy. He insisted that Sud Atlantique had received a copy of the report in November 1932, detailing the defects, and that they had failed in their duty to inform the insurers or to have the defects corrected.

He followed this up with yet another surprise: that very morning he had received a letter from M. Bertrand, the Minister of Merchant Marine, which detailed the cost of repairing and rebuilding *L'Atlantique*, and insisting that the liner must be regarded as uninsurable. This letter, the lawyer declaimed, was a blatant attempt by a Government Minister to influence the decision of the Court.

Following these sensational allegations, Maître Dor presented the response from Sud Atlantique on 30 November 1934. Not only did he refute all the allegations, he claimed that the agent representing the automatic pilot had put in two totally contradictory reports. Furthermore, at the time of the disaster the auto pilot had not even been connected, so any comments about it were irrelevant.

Maître Dor then returned to the terms clearly stated in the insurance contract – that if the cost of the repairs were more than the insured value, the owners had the right to hand the liner over to the insurers. The various experts appointed by the Court had agreed that this was the case. Maître Dor also challenged the interpretation put on the letter received from M. Bertrand, insisting that it was simply a statement from the Ministry to show that it had fully approved of the action for the abandonment of *L'Atlantique*.

The Court adjourned to consider the various arguments. On 14 December the Court reconvened, when it was addressed by the Advocate General, Maître Rollin, who found conclusively in favour of Sud Atlantique. Many felt that this was a biased verdict, owing as much to political expediency as it did to points of law.

Judgement was passed down on 28 December 1934, finding for the company and against the insurers. On 21 January 1935 the insurers announced that they were refusing to accept the liner.

The insurers decided to appeal, and instructed Maître de Moro-Giafferi and Maître Sarrazi to prepare a new case. M. Laurant, the magistrate at Cherbourg, agreed to re-examine the electrical installation, using a new team of experts.

M. Giafferi called a M. Jaouen, who had been the foreman at Penhoët in charge of the original electrical installation. He confirmed that he had reported defects in the wiring initially, and that he had found similar defects in the remaining wiring he had inspected on the hulk.

The lawyers then called in experts who had been over the wiring; they listed cracks in the sheathing, patches to the cables and other weak points. The damaged areas were sealed off by Court order, and it was agreed that a senior engineer should continue the investigations.

By now allegations had been made by other people, in particular regarding the electrical wiring. A new trial began at Bordeaux in February 1935, which was soon suspended while the judge called for a new commission to investigate the electrical installation and to study the cables etc. still on board the wreck.

A report in March stated that the electrical cables in question were not relevant to the source or the scene of the fire, since virtually no current would have been passing through them, at the time the fire started.

The insurers announced in April that because of the new trial and the ongoing investigations into the electrical installation, they did not consider themselves bound by the earlier court ruling.

On 4 April the insurers took the case to the Court of Cassation, appealing against the Appeal Court verdict. The lawyers claimed that, as Sud Atlantique was aware of the faults in the wiring and had failed to notify the insurers, the insurance was void, as the insurers may have chosen to decline the risk.

They asked for the Court to defer any decision until the electrical investigations were complete. The Court refused to delay its findings, and stated that the results of the criminal investigation were irrelevant.

They ignored the fact that the magistrate at Cherbourg was still looking into the failures of the electrical installation – he had ordered an examination of the system on 22 December, six days before the previous Court's decision! The magistrate had ordered a further examination on 25 and 26 February, which had apparently revealed further defects. The Court disregarded it all as irrelevant and unsurprisingly upheld the findings for Sud Atlantique.

Two pictures of the hulk as she lay alongside the Marine Terminal - a depressing sight to all who saw her.

The court then appointed M. Desforges, a leading maritime engineer, to examine the cabling and the earlier evidence relating to the electrical installation. By August he reported that he found nothing new to support the contention of the insurers.

Consequently in December 1935 the Appeals Court threw out the insurers' claims and upheld the previous rulings.

However, now that the initial matter had been finally resolved, Sud Atlantique had to sort out the various claims of the salvage companies involved in the rescue operation.

The original insurance contract on *L'Atlantique* had been very badly written. The company had borrowed heavily to build the ship, and the final cost had been 291 million francs. However the liner was only insured for 170 million francs in total, and the salvage companies had lodged claims totalling a further 50 million francs.

Eventually the insurers had to pay out to Sud Atlantique, the salvage companies, the Homet rent, and the various legal costs.

The only people who lost out were the sailors from *L'Atlantique*, who were not covered by the insurance. They lost all their clothing and personal possessions in the fire, and received nothing. In particular the families of those who died in the fire lost most.

Finally, after so many months of litigation and argument, the hulk was eased away from the quayside to begin her final voyage.

At last, in February 1936 the rusting decaying wreck was sold to Smith & Houston, a shipbreaker based at Port Glasgow in Scotland, for £57,000 pounds.

On 29 February 1936 *L'Atlantique* was finally towed out of Homet, and temporarily moored at the transatlantic quay, while the hull was checked for seaworthiness and prepared for the tow to Scotland.

The whole sad saga was succinctly summarised in an excellent editorial in the *Shipbuilding and Shipping Record* of 19 December 1935. It cut clearly through all the conflicting legal arguments and laid the bare facts out very clearly.

The judgment of the Supreme Court of France, dismissing the underwriters' appeal in the case of *L'Atlantique*, has ended, so far as can be foreseeen, one of the most sensational and one of the most unsatisfactory legal disputes ever brought to court over a contract of marine insurance. The vessel was very badly damaged by fire in January, 1933, while bound from Pauillac for Havre for repairs. She was towed into Cherbourg, where she was condemned by the Commercial Tribunal, and the owners tendered notice of abandonment to the underwriters, claiming a total loss. She was insured on a value of 100,120,000 fr. with *bonne arrivée* (total loss only) insurances of 70,000,000 fr.

Despite early inspired contradictions of trouble over the claim, it soon became apparent that trouble had arisen, and eventually the owners instituted proceedings before the Seine Tribunal. Underwriters contested the competence of this Court to try the case with regard to the total loss only insurances, which contained an arbitration clause, but this was overruled. The case then turned on the question of whether the vessel could be repaired for less than her insured value, a tender by an English firm being the underwriters' arguments that she could, but the Court appointed three experts to report on the matter, and eventually two of them reported that the vessel could not be repaired, the third holding that she could be repaired, but at a greater cost than her insured value. In the meantime, a "Criminal Inquiry" was opened to ascertain the cause of the fire.

The underwriters appealed to the Appeal Court of Paris, adding to their previous plea another, much more serious, to the effect that the vessel's electric wiring was defective and that the owners had knowledge of this. This plea amounted to one of "concealment of material fact" on the grounds that had the underwriters shared the knowledge which they alleged the owners possessed it would have influenced their judgment of the risk.

They were endeavouring to prove their point by evidence before the Criminal Inquiry, and they requested the Paris Tribunal to postpone judgment until the result of this inquiry was known. This request was refused on the grounds that it had already been decided that the fire was not of electrical origin, a ruling that created a very bad impression since it was known that fresh evidence with regard to alleged defective wiring was to be heard by the judge holding the Criminal Inquiry. By

giving judgment before the inquiry was concluded the Paris Court made it impossible to underwriters to take the case to the Supreme Court of France except on a point of law, but the refusal to delay judgment afforded underwriters the point of law on which to appeal, and the case was taken to the Cour de Cassation. Unfortunately, when the fresh evidence with regard to alleged defective wiring was heard before the Criminal Inquiry, an essential witness was prevented from giving evidence by a serious illness, but the judge would not delay until this witness had recovered and eventually reported that the fire was not due to an electrical cause. Underwriters have appealed to have the inquiry reopened in order that their essential witness may be heard, but the Cour de Cassation, by giving judgment before the result of the appeal is known, has created a *fait accompli*, thus throwing upon the underwriters the onus of circumventing an apparently irrevocable judgment if it so happens that their appeal is allowed and they are eventually successful in proving the truth of those allegations which, they maintain, they have not had a proper opportunity to justify.

More accustomed to the ultra-careful processes of the English courts than to the less strict manner in which litigation is conducted in France, the case has undoubtedly created an unfortunate impression, and yet the feeling in the marine insurance market is that it has served a very useful purpose. Since proceedings were commenced there has been no continuance of that series of fires which included the losses of the *Asia*, *Paul Lecat* and *Georges Philippar*, and of which that on *L'Atlantique* was the last. During the proceedings the French Minister of Marine issued new and more stringent regulations with regard to the electrical equipment of French passenger ships, and it is known that since the litigation commenced the existing regulations have been more strictly enforced. There is also reason to believe that as a result of the fire on *L'Atlantique* the fire-fighting and preventive equipment which had been designed for the *Normandie* was made even more effective than had originally been intended, which is saying much. Of course, the cost has been heavy, the expenses of litigation being added to the amount of the claim, but the case was fought in good faith and on principle, and if at times it took unexpected turns, nothing transpired during the proceedings to make underwriters alter the opinion upon which they originally founded their decision to resist the claim.

Finally, at 2.14pm on 6 March 1936 four Smit tugs, under the control of Captain Hoeven, took the wreck under tow, and began the long haul to the breaker's yard.

L'Atlantique, waiting to pass up the Clyde to the breakers, was moved well clear of the main channel on 24 March to ensure she did not impede the Queen Mary *as she passed on her way down the Clyde to start her long, illustrious career.*

On 13 March the convoy arrived off the Clyde, and waited for clearance to proceed up river. While anchored, *L'Atlantique* was passed by the world's newest ocean liner: Cunard's *Queen Mary* came down river from the shipbuilders, heading out to sea for her trials. As *Queen Mary* passed the sad spectacle, she courteously saluted her lost companion of the sea.

L'Atlantique *arrived at Greenock on 13 March 1936 under the control of the Dutch tugs* Ganges, Wittezee, Nordzee *and* Indus. *Here she was taken over by the Steele & Bennie tugs* Campaigner, Warrior, Chieftain *and* Wrestler, *seen below, for the final tow to the Smith & Houston yard.*

The end of the long haul – the sad remains of L'Atlantique *arrives off Port Glasgow, ready for demolition.*

With the loss of the *L'Atlantique*, Sud Atlantique was left with just *Massilia* to maintain its passenger and postal service contracts to South America. During the Second World War the liner was requisitioned by the French government and used as a troopship. Later *Massilia* was seized by the Germans on 21 August 1941, in Marseilles, and on 22 August 1944 she was scuttled at Estaque in an attempt to block the entrance to Bassin Mirabeau. At the end of the war, the wreck was demolished where she lay.

Throughout its history, Sud Atlantique was one of the unluckiest companies in the shipping world. From the start they suffered repeated financial problems, fires, collisions, accidents, sinkings and strandings, plus the usual wartime mishaps with mines and torpedoes.

The shipbreakers secured the hulk stern first to the shore, using a heavy chain attached to winches. They then proceeded to demolish her, working from the stern forwards: as the wreck lightened, they simply dragged the wreck further inshore.

Bibliography

Previously published books and research material play a vital rôle in any work such as this. The following books – and others too numerous to mention – have proved invaluable in the research involved in this present work.

Baker White, J.	*Sabotage is Suspected*	Evans Bros	1957
Bernadac, B.	*L'Incendie de L'Atlantique*	Marines éditions	1997
Braynard, F.O. & Miller, W.H.	*Fifty Famous Liners Vol. 3*	Patrick Stephens	1987
Vian, L.	*Arts décoratifs à bord des paquebots français*	Éditions Fonmare	

In particular acknowledgement must be given to the shipping magazines of the day, especially Shipbuilder, Sea Breezes *and* Shipbuilding & Shipping Record, *and the various national newspapers, without whose combined reporting and archives this record would not have been possible. All possible efforts have been made to identify owners of copyright of any photographs or other material used. The author apologises to anyone who feels they have not been suitably acknowledged, and if they care to contact him, with proof of their claim, they will be duly credited in any future editions.*

Author's Opinion

In spite of prolonged study of various reports, studies and informed comment, I have been unable to reach a satisfactory conclusion as to the reasons behind the abrupt loss of such a large, well-equipped modern liner. There were many unanswered questions, even after three years of legal arguments, tribunals and interviews. For example:

- Why had no earlier radio message been put out?

- Why was there such a conflict in evidence between Captain Schoofs and the radio operator?

- Why were there so many obvious errors in Captain Schoofs' published "Account of the Disaster"? (see page 72)

- How and where did the fire start at all, and did it in fact start in several different cabins?

- Why was the partition between the two prime cabins only slightly damaged by fire?

- Why did the purser disappear so quickly once he arrived at the dockside, and what happened to the patrol controller machine?

- What happened to the evidential paperwork 'acquired' by the investigators in Champagnolle?

- Why were the courts allowed to reach conclusions that would affect the decisions of other courts?

- Why were witnesses not allowed to give their evidence?

- Why did the Advocate General feel it necessary to address the Court, and in such apparently biased tones?

- Why were the apparent faults in the electrical wiring considered irrelevant and ignored?

None of these or many other similar doubts and questions were ever answered adequately, then or since, and there must be a lingering suspicion that perhaps the problems of the Depression on world-wide trade were a factor.

However, I must stress that these are purely my own feelings and suspicions. I leave the reader to draw their own conclusions.